MOM CRAFTS

MOM CRAFTS

DIY CRAFTS FOR THE EXPECTANT MOM

LARK
New York

New York

An Imprint of Sterling Publishing Co., Inc.
1166 Avenue of the Americas
New York, NY 10036

ISBN 978-1-4547-1014-1

Distributed in Canada by Sterling Publishing Co., Inc.
c/o Canadian Manda Group, 664 Annette Street
Toronto, Ontario, Canada M6S 2C8
Distributed in the United Kingdom by GMC Distribution Services
Castle Place, 166 High Street, Lewes, East Sussex, England BN7 1XU
Distributed in Australia by NewSouth Books
45 Beach Street, Coogee, NSW 2034, Australia

For information about custom editions, special sales, and premium and corporate purchases,
please contact Sterling Special Sales at 800-805-5489 or specialsales@sterlingpublishing.com.

Manufactured in China

2 4 6 8 10 9 7 5 3 1

www.larkcrafts.com
www.sterlingpublishing.com

Photography by Chris Bain
Pattern on page i used throughout the book © Artulina / Shutterstock
Image on page 2 © Africa Studio / Shutterstock
Design by Lorie Pagnozzi

CONTENTS

INTRODUCTION

The birth of a baby is a momentous occasion, and, very often, so are the preparations for the baby's arrival. Moms want to ensure they have the best items for their baby—they must be useful, practical, well made, and suited to their specific needs. Friends and family are usually on the lookout for special items as well, as they'll want to gift the new mom and her baby with the perfect gift. *Mom Crafts* offers 20 projects for the discerning mom, family, and friends who want to make something heartfelt and personal for mom and baby to both enjoy.

Perfect for beginners and seasoned crafters alike, this book includes a comprehensive basics section and step-by-step instructions with how-to illustrations.

The projects are split between three sections: *Mom*, *Baby*, and *Nursery*. In the *Mom* section, you'll find essential items for the expectant mother: Projects include a stylish, Modern Nursing Bag featuring multiple pockets and a vinyl interior for easy cleaning; a diaper-and-wipes clutch that doubles as a changing mat on the go; and a Lavender Eye Pillow to soothe and relax a sleep-deprived parent. The *Baby* section features a Tummy Time Floor Quilt in high-contrast patchwork with an adorable

smiling heart; a bib pattern that incorporates a section of beautifully embroidered heirloom fabric; and an adorable knitted booties and hat set in a strawberry pattern. The book closes with the *Nursery* section—a collection of beautiful, colorful items that add a personal touch to baby's room—all perfect projects for a family member or friend to make as a special, heartfelt baby shower gift. Each project will be a keepsake to treasure for years to come.

Each of the projects is fully customizable. You can choose your own fabrics in your favorite colors, add a custom embroidery pattern, or improvise an extra feature—such as an additional pocket or strap—to cater to your personal needs. That's the beauty of creating items: While you are welcome to construct each of these projects according to the specific directions, each project is also a springboard for a unique, handcrafted item of your very own.

Enjoy making these projects for the new little one in your life. You'll create an item that's useful, practical, and, most of all, special, as it was handmade with love.

BASIC TOOLS, MATERIALS & TECHNIQUES

This chapter provides an overview of all the tools, materials, and techniques you'll need to make the projects in this book. Since the projects span a variety of craft styles, you'll be working with an array of fabrics, stitches, needles, etc.! Feel free to refer back to this section while you're crafting in case you get stuck and need a little extra guidance.

Tools

You'll be working with a wide variety of tools—some you may already have at home, and some you may need to acquire. Here we'll describe the tools used frequently throughout so you know what to expect and how to plan your shopping accordingly.

ERASABLE FABRIC PEN, PENCIL, OR CHALK

Now you see it . . . now you don't. These marking tools aren't magic, but their lines do vanish once the job is done. Use a water-soluble fabric marker when marking sewing or cutting lines and embroidery designs. The ink will disappear with plain water. It's always best to test a marker on a fabric scrap since the dyes in some fabrics can make the ink hard to remove. Tailor's chalk leaves dust on the surface of the fibers, but you'll find it easy to brush the marks away once they've served their purpose.

IRON

Hot, hot, hot! The secret's out: Irons aren't just for getting rid of wrinkles. This invaluable tool also sets seams and hems, and it applies heat to fusible web, transfers, and appliqués.

FLEXIBLE TAPE MEASURE AND TRANSPARENT RULER

Somehow it just doesn't feel like you're sewing unless you have a tape measure curled on the cutting table or draped around your neck, ready to measure on command. But a transparent ruler can't be beat for drawing a straight line or marking small measurements—a must-have when making these projects. You can also use the ruler as a straight edge when using a rotary cutter.

EMBROIDERY NEEDLES

Some projects call for an embroidery needle, which has a longer eye to accommodate thicker embroidery floss.

HAND-SEWING NEEDLES

A variety pack of needles is all you need to handle the general sewing in the projects of this book. The range of needle sizes allows you to sew together most common fabrics.

SEWING MACHINE NEEDLES

Grrr! Broken needle! Dull needle! Need we say more? Except that the *real* frustration comes when you find you don't have extras on hand. Machine needles are inexpensive, and it pays to purchase several packs at a time. Give yourself a gift by getting in the habit of starting each project with a new needle; it has to be one of life's most economical luxuries. Go ahead and indulge. And don't forget to pick up a few specialty needles for your sewing machine, like round-tipped needles for stretch fabrics and leather needles for heavier vinyl fabrics.

NEEDLE THREADER

You think you have it, only to find you've missed the mark. Then you try again. Attempting to thread a needle over and over doesn't do much for your self-esteem. Save yourself the trouble by using a needle threader. Simply push the thin wire loop of this tiny tool through the eye of a needle, insert the thread, and pull the loop out.

PINKING SHEARS

The zigzag pattern made by pinking shears prevents fabric from fraying. Use them to trim a seam or add a decorative touch to any edge.

PINS

Traditional, short metal pins with small heads will do the job, but they're no fun. The longer pins with plastic or glass heads are easier to handle and can make pinning a more colorful experience.

SEAM RIPPER

A seam ripper is probably the most satisfying of all sewing supplies to own because it can undo mistakes in no time. Like the perfect gift, it keeps on giving by continually providing you with a second (or third, or fourth!) chance at perfection.

SEWING MACHINE

Several of these projects require a sewing machine. Even if you're an experienced seamstress, a quick review of the most basic rules for machine stitching can help you as you work. For example, when sewing thicker fabrics, make sure to reduce the pressure on the foot and use a longer stitch—this simple step allows the fabric to glide through the feeder. For any seam that needs a good anchor, Backstitch at the beginning and end of the seam to secure the stitching. Use the Zigzag Stitch on raw edges to prevent the fabric from fraying. Change the presser foot as needed for the task at hand whenever you are Straight Stitching, Zigzagging, or applying a zipper. (For information on stitches, turn to the Stitch Gallery on page 23.)

ROTARY CUTTER AND MAT

Quilters popularized rotary cutters because their sharp rolling wheels quickly slice through multiple layers of fabric. Now crafters use them for many of their fabric-cutting needs. You'll find that some projects substitute this tool for scissors. If you choose to use a rotary cutter, always use it with a self-healing mat. Aside from saving your work surface, the mat has a printed grid that provides an extra measure of accuracy when you cut.

CRAFT SCISSORS

Reach for these scissors when cutting anything *but* fabric. An all-purpose pair should be of a moderate length for ease of use when cutting out curves and corners on paper patterns and templates. Don't break the bank when purchasing these scissors. In fact, you might already have more pairs lurking about than you dare admit.

EMBROIDERY SCISSORS

A welcome addition to any sewing basket is a good pair of fine-tipped scissors, such as embroidery scissors. They quickly slip into smaller spaces, making them easy to maneuver when clipping tight curves or doing tiny detail work.

SEWING SCISSORS

Save these scissors for fabric only. Using them to cut paper will dull the blades, making them useless on fabric. If you're shopping for a new pair, quality is worth the extra cost. Give the scissors a test run at the store before purchasing them. If they fit comfortably in your grip as you snip, you'll be assured a lifetime of happy cutting.

ON PERFECT CORNERS

After sewing and trimming a corner, it's time to turn the fabric right-side out. Wait a minute. . . . The corner still looks all bunched up. What to do? Grab a chopstick or knitting needle! Use it to push the corner out before pressing, and you'll be done in no time with perfect results.

Assorted Tools and Materials

Some of these projects employ tools and materials that are only used once or twice, so we've separated these out into their own section.

ACRYLIC PAINT

What's not to love about acrylic paint? It's easily found at any craft store, inexpensive, water soluble, and dries quickly! It's hard not to have a rainbow of colors in your craft stash.

EMBROIDERY HOOP

Two simple wooden circles, one inside the other, hold fabric taut when you need to embroider. This can be used repeatedly to hold your fabric while embroidering, or you can use it as a frame for your embroidery, like in the Playful Embroidered Pencil Hoop Art on page 87.

FLORAL WIRE

Floral wire is available in a variety of thicknesses depending on how you want to use it. For the Yarn-Wrapped Name Sign on page 107, you'll be working with a 16-gauge, vine-coated wire, which is wide enough to prominently spell out a child's name while still being pliable enough to bend.

HAMMER

Typically used in woodworking crafts, any small hammer will do. You'll need a small hammer to secure the upholstery tacks in the Elegant Footprint Plaque on page 105.

HOT GLUE GUN AND CARTRIDGES

When you're looking for a fast and secure seal, working with a hot glue gun and glue cartridges is a popular solution. Each solid stick of glue is melted and extruded through the gun, which you control with a trigger. Just be very careful never to touch the tip of your hot glue gun when it's plugged in, because you can burn yourself easily. Keep some newspaper handy when not using the hot glue gun since glue can drip out from the nozzle.

GLUE STICK

Glue sticks are a great all-purpose, washable adhesive option. They work best on paper, whereas hot glue can be used on a wider variety of materials.

PLIERS AND WIRE CUTTERS

There are a wide array of pliers that perform specific actions, but in general pliers are used for grasping and bending objects, as seen in the Yarn-Wrapped Name Sign on page 107. The biggest difference between pliers and wire cutters is that wire cutters are used to sever wire, as opposed to grabbing or turning.

PAINTBRUSHES AND PAINT TRAY

Paintbrushes made with manmade materials are typically inexpensive, whereas paintbrushes that use animal fibers are more costly. There are many brush tips that serve a variety of purposes in terms of painting wide areas versus painting fine details. For the purpose of the projects in this book, a paintbrush with a flat or bright tip will get the job done. A paint tray allows you to mix colors together in case you want to blend for a unique shade or effect.

INK PAD

Ink pads come in a wide range of colors and sizes depending on the stamping project you have in mind. For the Elegant Footprint Plaque on page 105, you'll just want to make sure you choose a pad that fits your baby's foot on its surface and pick a color that contrasts well with the paint you use on the plaque.

UPHOLSTERY TACKS

Upholstery tacks are typically used for securing fabric when reupholstering furniture and can also be used for other decorative purposes, such as in the Elegant Footprint Plaque on page 105.

WOODEN PLAQUE

You can find blank, premade wooden plaques in the woodworking section of most chain craft stores. You'll have a variety of shapes to choose from, such as ovals, circles, squares, and sometimes hearts, so pick the shape that makes you happy.

Materials

From fabrics to hardware to embroidery threads—we cover all your most-used materials here.

BIAS TAPE

Bias tape is made from strips of fabric cut on the bias (diagonal) rather than the straight of the grain. This gives the tape the perfect amount of stretch for skirting corners and curves when binding raw edges. You can purchase single-fold or double-fold bias tape in various widths (blanket binding is extra wide) and in an almost infinite range of colors. You can also customize your project by making your own contrasting or coordinating bias tape (page 11). It's easy!

BLACK NO. 8 PERLE COTTON

Perle cotton (or pearl cotton) is a 2-ply twisted thread that is recognizable for its shine and for being non-divisible, meaning the plies do not split or kink. It's used for a variety of needlework projects, including appliqué, crochet, embroidery, cross-stitch, and needlepoint, among other crafts.

BUTTONS, EYELETS, AND SNAPS

Even though each of these small notions serves a purpose, they can do double duty as beautiful embellishments. In other words, why settle for plain when the world is full of fabulous, decorative buttons? Same for snaps—in the time it takes you to sew one, you could apply an even snappier version. And eyelets (also called grommets), those humble little metal circles, carry a drawstring with a bit more cachet than a buttonhole.

FABRIC GLUE

Fabric glue is especially useful for attaching accessories to fabric without sewing. In the Bitty Bear Diaper Bag Tag on page 73, you'll use it to adhere a hook-and-loop closure without sewing.

FLOSSES

The projects that include embroidery embellishments will need multi-strand embroidery floss in cotton, silk, or rayon.

FRAY RETARDANT

A product that binds with fibers to prevent unraveling, fray retardant comes in both liquid and spray-on applications. Use it when you find yourself in a tight spot, like when you're unable to zigzag a seam, or anytime you want to seal raw edges, as for appliqués.

FUSIBLE WEB

Some inventions are truly a gift from the universe. The versatile no-sew alternative for affixing fabric to fabric uses a heat-activated adhesive. Paper-backed fusible web, much like double-sided tape, lets you adhere two surfaces, making it the perfect material for crafting and applying appliqués with ease.

HARDWARE

D-rings, split rings (commonly called key rings), and magnets are essential bits of hardware when you're looking to make the right attachments. You can find these at craft or sewing stores or online.

HOOK-AND-LOOP CLOSURE

Also called hook-and-loop fasteners or tape, these are generally made up of two parts: two matching strips that "catch" one another. One strip has a soft, "hairy" surface, and the other has a series of tiny hooks that catch onto the hairy side and are more scratchy. Press these two strips together and they magically and temporarily adhere! You'll just want to be careful that the scratchy side isn't placed to come in contact with your baby's delicate skin.

INTERFACING

Interfacing adds support and structure to your sewn presents. It comes in different weights, but most projects use light- or medium-weight interfacing for subtle shaping. For projects that have to retain their shape, you'll need a much stiffer, heavier weight of interfacing. Fusible interfacing, applied with an iron, works well on most fabrics. Avoid using it on velvet or corduroy, however, because the iron will crush the nap.

LAYERING AND STUFFING MATERIALS

Flannel, cotton batting, or fusible fleece provide a soft touch to any project that needs a cushioning layer between fabrics. Fusible fleece adds a padded layer to your sewing project. When used in the Diaper Change Mat Clutch (page 45), it adds a little padding for a baby's comfort. Fusible fleece has adhesive on one side (and sometimes both sides), which eliminates the need for basting (pinning, tacking, or spray-gluing layers of fabric together before sewing or quilting). When making pillows, you'll discover that precut foam forms in just the right size will always fill your needs, like for the Whale Pillow & Photo Prop on page 95. For stuffing shapes, such as the Maternity Pillow on page 51, polyester fiberfill is the all-around favorite material of choice . . . unless, of course, you decide to make the Lavender Eye Pillow on page 29, which is full of rice.

MASKING TAPE

What makes masking tape special is that it's easy to tear and easy to peel off. While it's mainly used to mask off areas that should not be painted, it's an easy-to-use tape with a variety of purposes.

THREADS

You can't go wrong with choosing a quality polyester thread for all-purpose machine- and hand-sewing. This versatile thread sews strong seams, which is essential for projects designed to hold items.

TRACING PAPER OR TISSUE PAPER

This thin paper is transparent enough for you to see through it and trace a design. You can use this for an embroidery technique: Copy a design onto the tracing paper, pin it to your embroidery fabric, and then embroider directly through the tracing paper, using the sketched design as a guide. Because the paper is very thin, it can easily be torn away once your embroidery is complete.

ZIPPERS

The Modern Nursing Bag on page 31 will need a zipper to keep all of the contents safe and secure. Nylon zippers are less bulky than metal ones, but you may opt for a metal zipper—a sturdy and durable choice. Zippers come in a variety of lengths and are easy to apply using a standard Running Stich application (page 25).

Fabric

COTTON

Is there anything this fabric can't do? The different weights—from gossamer to canvas—fill many needs. Medium-weight cotton is suitable for making many of the projects in this book. It's easy to sew and comes in a wide variety of colors and patterns. Choose one you love.

Fat Quarters

A fat quarter is a ½-yard (.45-m) cut of fabric that has then been cut in half again to make a piece measuring 18 x 21 inches (45.7 x 53.3 cm). You may know them more commonly as those irresistible little bundles of colorful fabric you see in shops. They're the perfect size for making small gifts, so buy an assortment.

Fat Eighths

A fat eighth is a ¼-yard (.91-m) cut of fabric that has then been cut in half to make a piece measuring 9 x 21 inches (22.8 x 53.3 cm). Otherwise known as half of a fat quarter.

FELT

What's soft, doesn't fray or ravel, has no right or wrong side, and is available for purchase in just about any sewing or craft supply store? Felt, of course. No wonder it's every crafter's favorite fabric. Traditionally felt is made of wool, though the squares or bolts of felt you find in stores are likely made from synthetic fibers.

FLEECE

Fleece is easy to sew and durable, as well as washable and quick-drying. But its biggest appeal is its inviting, plush texture. Use it for cuddly baby gifts or whenever you want to make someone a present that feels like a hug.

LINEN

The word "crisp" comes to mind when we think of linen, as do the words "lustrous" and "beautiful." Use it when you need a durable fabric that has a bit of body to it. (Hint: It's a classic fabric for making napkins!) Linen does wrinkle, so iron it often before, during, and after sewing to keep it smooth.

PLUSH MICROFIBER

Plush microfiber fabric is manufactured to feel like real mink to the touch. With a short pile and as soft as cashmere, plush microfiber is perfect for creating baby clothes and accessories. Use it to back a blanket or a bib, as in the Embroidered Linen Bib (page 75), for a super-soft side that will be comforting for any baby.

STRETCH KNIT

Two clear advantages to stretch knit are that (1) it's durable and (2) it has a lot of give. Generally made from polyester, cotton, and/or wool combined with spandex, stretch knits are widely available.

UPHOLSTERY OR HOME DECOR FABRICS

These fabrics are in a category all their own—but don't let that stop you. Even if you aren't covering a sofa or sewing drapes, you can still use these fabrics for the hard-wearing projects in this book. The wide array of textures, colors, and patterns available in natural fibers, synthetics, and blends is worth a look.

WOOL

Classic and classy, wool endures as a favorite sewing fabric. Just a small touch provides texture and charm.

VINYL

Clear vinyl is essential when making presents with see-through pockets or windows. You can purchase vinyl off the bolt at a fabric store, or you can trim a bit off an old, clear vinyl tablecloth (just make sure no one's watching!).

Techniques

This section contains the basic sewing know-how you'll need to make all the beautiful projects in this book. If you're a beginner, use the section to learn something new. For those more experienced crafters, give this a quick review. You'll know what to expect and can get right to work.

BINDING WITH BIAS TAPE

Bias tape binds raw edges for a finished look. When you have a project that has straight edges and corners, follow the instructions on this page for binding with mitered corners. (For a how-to on making bias tape, see page 14.)

BINDING WITH MITERED CORNERS

1. Measure the length of the edge to bind, and then add an extra couple of inches for folding under the raw ends and overlapping.

2. Open the tape and fold one of the ends under. With right sides together and raw edges aligned, sew the tape to the fabric. Stop sewing ¼ inch (6 mm) from the corner, and then fold the binding over itself to create a crease (figure 1).

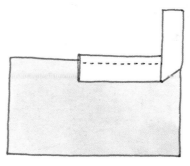

figure 1

3. Fold the binding down and rotate the fabric 90 degrees. Don't stitch across the corner, but instead stitch ¼ inch (6 mm) in from the edge (figure 2), sewing down toward the next corner. Continue stitching around the edges and mitering the corners in this way until you get back to your starting point.

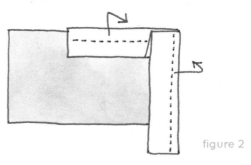

figure 2

4. Fold the loose end under to overlap the starting point by 1 inch (2.5 cm), trimming the end first if necessary to reduce the bulk. Then complete stitching the seam. Fold the binding over the seam allowance to the other side of the fabric. Fold the edges of the corners in as you would if wrapping a package (figure 3), and then Ladder Stich the binding to the other side of the fabric. This gives a very nice finish to the Tummy Time Floor Quilt (page 65).

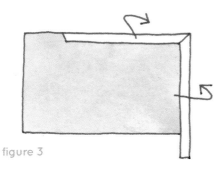

figure 3

CLIPPING CORNERS

When you turn a corner right-side out, the excess fabric can bunch in the seams, creating ugly lumps and bumps. But don't worry. A few well-placed snips and clips can smooth your work to perfection.

After sewing, cut the seam allowance at a 45-degree angle to the raw edge. Cut close to the stitching but be careful to avoid cutting the stitches (figure 4).

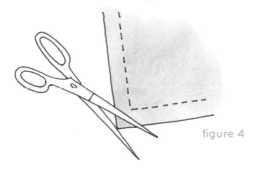

figure 4

CLIPPING OR NOTCHING CURVES

Just like corners, sewn curves need some attention, too. You *clip* an inward curve but *notch* an outward curve. To clip an inward curve, use scissors to cut into the seam allowance at several places around the curve (figure 5). Don't clip too close since you don't want to cut into the stitching. To notch an outward curve, cut small V-shaped wedges from the seam allowance (figure 6), being careful to avoid cutting into the stitching.

figure 5

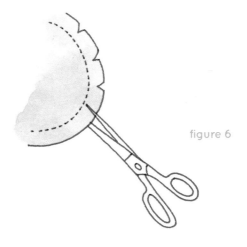

figure 6

EMBROIDERY TRANSFER METHOD

For patterns with embroidery designs, enlarge the template to the appropriate size, and then trace the template (including any embroidery patterns) onto a piece of tissue paper. Pin the tissue paper in place on the fabric to be embroidered. Embroider the designs (through both the fabric and the paper). When finished, tear away the tissue paper. You may need to use a sewing needle or tweezers to pull out any tiny pieces stuck under your stitches.

MACHINE STITCHING

First, test the tension of your machine by stitching on a scrap of the fabric you'll be using; you want the stitches to be smooth on both sides. If necessary, follow the instructions in your machine's manual to adjust the tension for the top thread or the bobbin. When you're ready, follow these steps to sew the perfect seam.

1. Pin the fabric pieces together using straight pins placed at right angles to the seam. Unless the project instructions tell you otherwise, most seams are sewn with right sides together and raw edges aligned.

2. As you sew, pull the pins out before they reach the needle. Be quick! If you're too late, the machine needle can nick the pins, making them unusable, or can dull or break the needle itself.

3. Pivoting the fabric when sewing a corner will give you a perfect sharp angle. When you get to the corner point, stop with the needle down in the fabric. Then lift the presser foot, turn the fabric, lower the presser foot, and merrily sew on your way.

4. Give it up! Let the machine do the work of pulling the fabric through as you sew. This simple exercise can save you uneven stitches, stretched fabric, and puckered seams.

MAKING AND ATTACHING STRAPS

A strap handle, like the one on the Modern Nursing Bag (page 31), is quick and easy to make and attach. Start with a straight strip of fabric. Fold the two long raw edges under, wrong sides together, to make narrow hems, and press (figure 7). Fold the strip in half lengthwise, aligning the edges, and press in the crease. Topstitch both long sides of the strap (figure 8). Pin the right sides of the strap to the right sides of the bag (figure 9), and you're ready to sew them into the seam of the binding or lining.

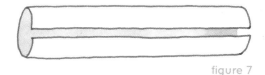

figure 7

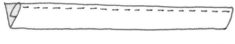

figure 8

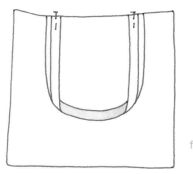

figure 9

MAKING BIAS TAPE

To get a coordinated, custom look, make your own bias tape. It's easier than you might think, and it adds *sew* much more to every gift.

1. Cut strips four times as wide as your desired tape on lines running 45 degrees to the selvage (figure 10).

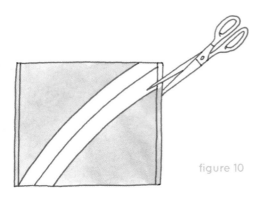

figure 10

2. Piece the strips by laying one strip over another, with right sides together and at right angles. Pin them together, and then stitch diagonally across the corners of the overlapping squares (figure 11). Cut off the corners, leaving a ¼-inch (6-mm) seam allowance.

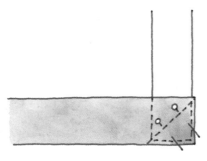

figure 11

3. Open the seams and press the seam allowances flat. Fold the strip in half lengthwise, wrong sides together, and press again. Open the strip and press the raw edges into the center. This makes single-fold bias tape (figure 12).

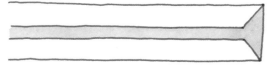

figure 12

4. To make double-fold bias tape, fold the strip into the center once more and press (figure 13).

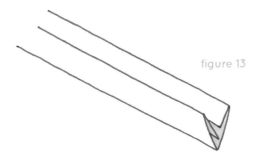

figure 13

PIECING

Piecing, also known as patchwork, is a method of sewing small sections of fabric together to produce a certain pattern or quilt block. Cutting your fabric accurately and using an exact standard seam allowance of ¼ inch (6 mm) are key factors for successful piecing. For perfect piecing, start by pinning the first fabric cuts with right sides together. Stitch along the edge using the desired seam allowance. Add more pieces in the same way to make a row. When one row is complete, make another. Then pin and sew the rows together.

PRESSING SEAMS

Pressing the seams of a project helps it look its best—your seams will be crisp and neat, and it will be easier to work with the fabric. Be sure to test your iron on a small piece of the fabric you will be pressing before working on the actual project. Start with the iron set to a low heat setting—too high, and the iron may leave a mark or melt the fabric. As a precaution, lay a lightweight pressing cloth (cotton, muslin, or a tea towel) over the project as you iron it. Pick up and press down on the iron as you move down the length of the seam, and use your fingers to hold the seam open. Take your time to avoid burning your fingers!

QUILTING

Quilting creates a padded, textured fabric, which is both practical and decorative. It's made by sandwiching batting between two layers of fabric and then stitching the layers together by machine or by hand using a Running Stitch. Before stitching, place pins or sew long Basting Stitches to hold the layers and prevent them from shifting.

STRETCH MARKINGS

A few of the projects in this book mention "stretch markings," like the Rainbow Baby Sling (page 59). Fabrics generally have more stretch when pulled in one direction than the other. Be sure to position the fabric according to the direction of the greatest stretch before cutting.

SEAM ALLOWANCES

A seam allowance is the space between a line of stitching and the edge of the fabric. Most of the projects in this book will specify a certain seam allowance to keep in mind when cutting templates and sewing. Check your project's instructions for its specific seam allowance—most will be ¼ inch (6 mm).

USING TEMPLATES

The templates for each project are organized in the back of this book (page 110). Each template notes the percentage at which the template should be enlarged and copied from the book to be rendered at full size for each project. There are several ways to transfer the templates from the book to paper and then finally to your project.

When printing templates from the book, be sure to set your printer to "actual size" or "size to 100%." Do not select the "fit to page" setting. If you do not have a printer, visit your local copy shop for help with printing the template at the correct size.

Once your template is printed, use an erasable fabric marker, pen, or chalk to trace the template's shape onto your fabric. Be sure to incorporate space for seam allowances as specified in each project's instructions. You can also use straight pins to pin the template in place as you cut the template piece away from the larger piece of fabric.

KNITTING

Since knitting has its own vocabulary, we've separated out its specific tools, materials, and techniques into this one handy section.

Needles

Knitting needles come in three varieties: straight needles, circular needles, and double-pointed needles. Straight needles have a pointed end and a blunt end with a stopper to keep stitches from sliding off the needles. This is used for projects where your knitting is worked flat. Circular needles have two pointed ends connected by a cord and are used primarily for projects that are worked in the round, but can also be used for knitting flat. Double-pointed needles have two pointed ends and are also used for working in the round.

Stitch Holder

When you need to pause a section of your knitting project, you can slide your stitches on to a stitch holder. Stitch holders look like an oversized safety pin and come in a variety of sizes based on how many stitches you need to put on hold.

Stitch Markers

Think of these like a bookmark for knitting! Stitch markers are tiny rings that you slip on to your knitting needle at a specific location to remind you of something—that this spot is the beginning of the round or that you should increase or decrease.

Tapestry Needle

This blunt-tipped sewing needle is used to weave in ends on your knitting projects. The round tip of the needle doesn't split the yarn as you weave, and the eye of the needle is large enough to accommodate the thickness of your yarn.

Yarn

Wool? Superwash wool? Cotton? Acrylic? Cashmere? A wool/cotton/acrylic blend? Take your pick, because there are so many fiber options and a variety of yarn weights for you to choose from. For a baby knit, you may want to choose a machine-washable material, like superwash wool, or you may want something a little less toothy for a baby's delicate skin, like a wool/cotton blend.

KNITTING TECHNIQUES

Bind-Off (BO)

The basic knit bind off is a great all-purpose method to learn. Knit two stitches. * With the tip of your left-hand needle, pull the second stitch on the right-hand needle over the first (figure 14) and let it drop off. You'll now have one stitch left on the needle (figure 15). Knit another stitch and repeat from * (figure 16). Continue in this manner, or as the pattern directs, until you have one stitch remaining on the left-hand needle. Cut off the yarn and pull the tail through the last stitch to fasten off.

> ✻ NOTE: *Knitting patterns often repeat a series of steps across an entire row. Asterisks (*) indicate that you should repeat the directions until you reach the end of the row.*

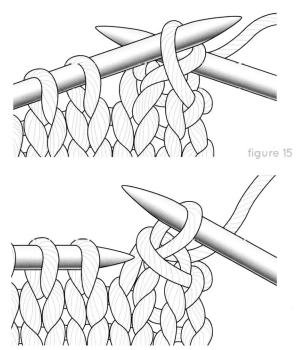

figure 15

figure 16

Cast On (CO)

The longtail cast on is a good all-purpose cast on method. Calculate about 1 inch (2.5 cm) of yarn per stitch that you'll be casting on; this will be your tail. Letting the tail hang, tie a slipknot around one of your knitting needles. You'll now have two strands of yarn hanging down from your needle—the tail, and the strand connected to the ball (figure 17). Placing the needle in your right hand, separate the two strands of yarn with your left thumb and index finger. Secure both loose ends under your ring finger and pinky (figure 18). Use your needle to scoop under the outer strand of the thumb loop (figure 19), then over the inner strand of the index finger loop (figure 20). Let the loop fall off your thumb (figure 21), and pull the tail so the stitch fits loosely onto your needle. Repeat until you've cast on the desired number of stitches.

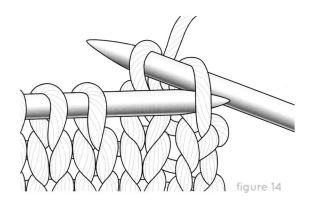

figure 14

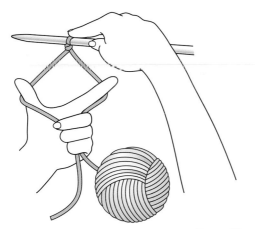

figure 17

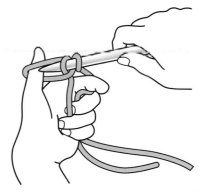

figure 20

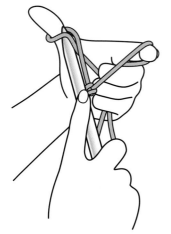

figure 18

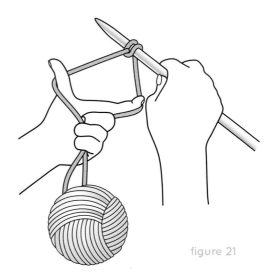

figure 21

figure 19

Picot Cast On

A picot cast on adds lovely detail to an otherwise simple knitting project and is completely customizable—you can add different numbers of stitches and numbers cast on to make longer or shorter tails. Just be sure to keep track of your stitches! Use knit stitch to cast on however many stitches are needed for your project before the first picot tail, then add stitches for the picot tail (figure 22). * Knit the first two tail stitches (figure 23). Bind off one stitch (figure 24), then knit and bind off two additional stitches. These three bound-off stitches are the picot tail. The stitch on the right-hand needle is a cast on for the edge. Slip it onto the left-hand needle (figure 25). Cast on however many stitches your project dictates before the next picot tail, along with the number of stitches needed for the tail. Repeat from * until the correct number of stitches are cast on to the left-hand kneedle (figure 26).

figure 25

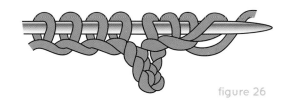

figure 26

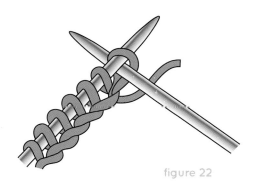

figure 22

Knit Stitch (K)

For the knit stitch, hold the needle with stitches on it in your left hand, and hold the working yarn in your right hand and at the back of the work. Insert the right-hand needle, from bottom to top, into the stitch as shown on the followig page (figure 27). The tips of the needles will form an X. Use your right index finger to wrap the strand of yarn counterclockwise around the right-hand needle (figure 28). Bring the yarn through the stitch with the right-hand needle and pull the loop off the left-hand needle (figure 29). You now have one complete knit stitch on your right-hand needle. Continue until the end of the row or as the pattern directs.

figure 23

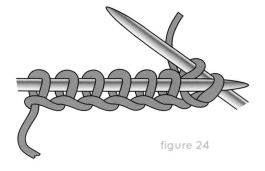

figure 24

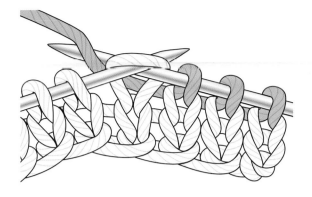

figure 27

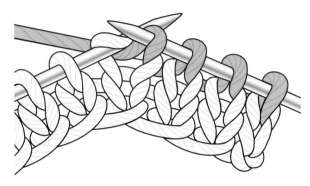

figure 28

figure 29

Mattress Stitch

Place pieces to be seamed side by side with right sides facing you. Using a tapestry needle, insert needle under the first bar on the edge of one piece of fabric. Insert the needle under the

first bar of the second piece of fabric. Continue in this way, matching the bars, until the entire seam has been completed (figure 30).

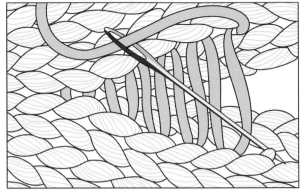

figure 30

Purl Stitch (P)

For the purl stitch, hold the needle with the stitches on it in your left hand. Hold the working yarn in your right hand and at the front of your work. Insert the right-hand needle, from top to bottom, into the stitch (figure 31). Using your right index finger, wrap the strand of yarn counterclockwise around the right-hand needle (figure 32). Bring the yarn through the stitch with the right-hand needle, and pull the loop off the left-hand needle (figure 33). Continue until the end of the row or as the pattern directs.

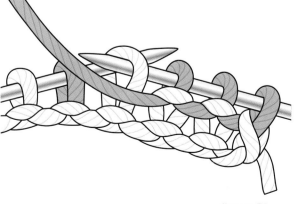

figure 31

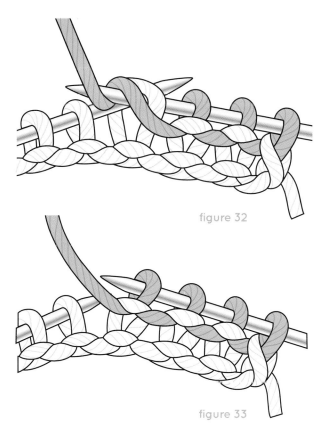

figure 32

figure 33

Decrease: k2tog

Insert needle into the next two stitches on the left-hand needle as if to knit. Knit both stitches together as if they are one (figure 35).

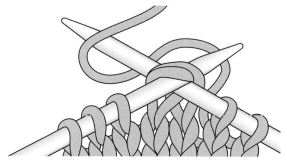

figure 35

Slip, Slip, Knit (SSK)

Slip your next two stitches, one at a time, onto the right-hand needle (figure 36). Insert the tip of the left-hand needle into the fronts of these stitches (figure 37), from left to right, and knit them together.

Purl Two Together (P2tog)

Insert needle into the next two stitches on the left-hand needles as if to purl. Purl both stitches together as if they were one (figure 34).

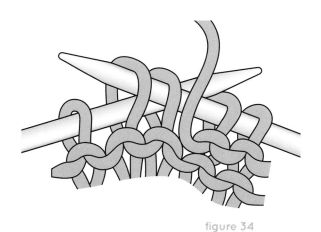

figure 34

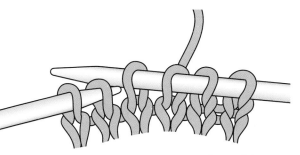

figure 36

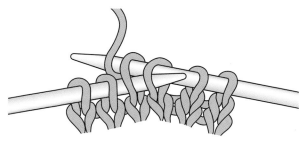

figure 37

Increases (Incr)

Make one left: Insert left-hand needle from the front to the back under the horizontal strand between the stitch just worked and the next stitch (figure 38). Knit the lifted strand through the back loop (figure 39).

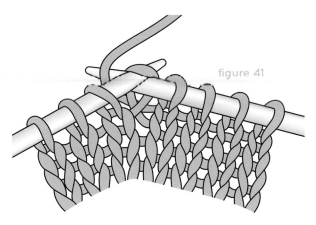

figure 41

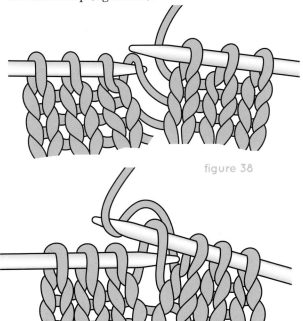

figure 38

figure 39

Make one right: Insert left-hand needle from back to front under the horizontal strand between the stitch just worked and the next stitch (figure 40). Knit the lifted strand through the front loop (figure 41).

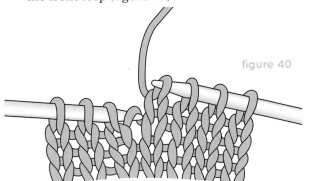

figure 40

Stockinette Stitch (St st)

Stockinette stitch combines knit stitch and purl stitch in alternate rows. The rows and columns interlock in V shapes throughout and create a smooth background.

KNITTING ABBREVIATIONS

BO	bind off
CO	cast on
Decr	decrease
Incr	increase
K	knit
K2tog	knit two together
P	purl
P2tog	purl two together
Rep	repeat
Rnd(s)	round(s)
RS	right side
SSK	slip, slip, knit
St(s)	stitch(es)
St st	stockinette stitch
WS	wrong side

HAND-SEWING STITCHES

BACKSTITCH

To create a Backstitch, start a Running Stitch from point A to B, then bring your needle back through the fabric a short distance away at point C. End by bringing your needle through at point A again (figure 42).

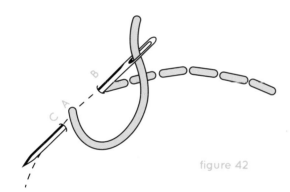

figure 42

BASTING STITCH

A Basting Stitch (or tacking stitch) is a temporary stitch used to hold pieces of fabric in place. To Baste, simply create long Running Stitches (see following page). Once your main stitching has been completed, carefully remove the Basting Stitches with a seam ripper.

BLANKET STITCH

Blanket Stitch (figure 43) is a pretty, decorative stitch for borders or edges. Push your needle in through the back of the fabric, close to the fabric's edge. Make a loose, diagonal stitch from point A to point B. Bring the needle up again at point C, catching the loose thread under the needle as you make the parallel stitches.

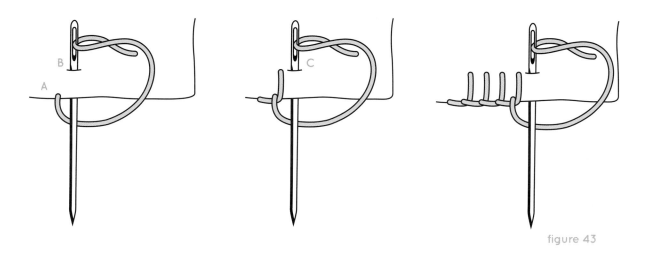

figure 43

LADDER STITCH

Ladder Stitch, also known as Blind or Hidden Stitch, is a nearly invisible stitch perfect for sewing seams (figure 44). To Ladder Stitch, bring the needle and thread through the back of the fabric at point A and then back down across the opening at point B. Slide the needle along the opening between the two pieces of fabric and pull it out at point C. Reinsert the needle at point D and then pull lightly. Continue along the opening to close the seam.

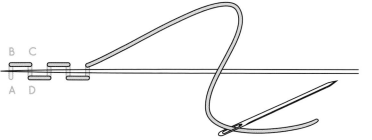

figure 44

RUNNING STITCH

Also known as Straight Stitch, Running Stitch is very simple. Use a loose Running Stitch to keep pieces of fabric in place as you work (figure 45). Push your needle and thread through the back of the fabric at point A, then push back down at point B, up at point C, and then down at point D; continue.

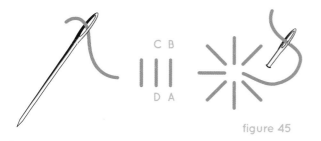

figure 45

WHIP STITCH

To Whip Stitch, simply sew over and around the edges of two pieces of fabric to create a seam (figure 46). Hold the two pieces together or pin them in place with straight pins as you sew.

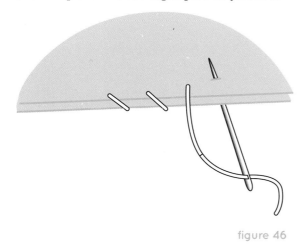

figure 46

SEWING MACHINE STITCHES

TOPSTITCH

A Topstitch is sewn parallel to a seam or along a hem on the right side of the fabric. It is the most common of sewing machine stitches.

EDGESTITCH

Edgestitching is simply Topstitching that hugs the edge of a seam. Make it the same way as topstitching, except sew as close to the edge as possible.

ZIGZAG STITCH

Zigzag Stich is a common back-and-forth sewing machine stitch, perfect for finishing the edges of seam allowances.

EMBROIDERY STITCHES

FRENCH KNOT

To create a French Knot, bring your needle up through the fabric in the exact spot where you would like the knot to appear. Pull the thread through until your finishing knot is flush against the backside of the fabric. Wrap the thread over and around the mid-section of the needle three or four times, keeping the needle's head close to the surface of the fabric. Slide the looped thread down the needle so it's close to the tip, then push the needle back into the cloth, close to where the needle came up. Pinch the loops in place as you push the needle down through the fabric. Pull the needle completely through, and the French Knot will form on the front of the fabric (figure 47).

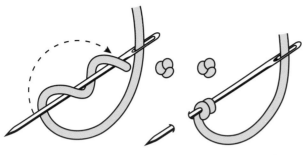

figure 47

SATIN STITCH

To Satin Stitch, bring your needle and thread up through the back of the fabric. Make a Straight Stitch, then another directly next to it, a little longer or shorter as needed. Continue this process until you have filled the space with parallel stitches to create a smooth, raised grouping of stitches (figure 48). Draw the desired template onto your fabric with a fine-tip fabric pen to use as a guide when filling the shape in with your Satin Stitches.

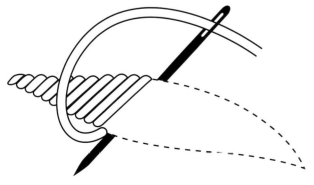

figure 48

SCALLOP STITCH

Scallop Stitches are great for making flowers or leaves, or you can stitch several in a row to make a pretty border. Make a loose stitch from A to B and press it flat to one side with your finger. Bring the needle to the front of the fabric at C, inside the loop. Insert the needle at the outside of the stitch, at D, to hold it in place (figure 49).

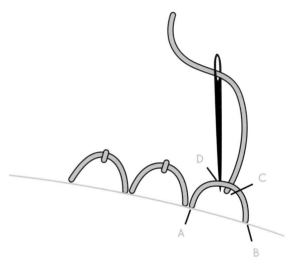

figure 49

MOM

LAVENDER EYE PILLOW

DESIGNER ✖ JESSICA FEDIW

A relaxing and sweet-smelling treat, this lavender eye pillow is the perfect accessory for a sleep-deprived mom. Place the eye pillow in the freezer or refrigerator before placing on tired eyes, or heat in the microwave for 30 seconds and place on forehead to aid in headache relief.

MATERIALS & TOOLS

✖ 3 pieces of fabric for the front, each 4 x 5 inches (10.2 x 12.7 cm)

✖ Scissors

✖ Pins

✖ Sewing machine and supplies

✖ Iron

✖ 1 piece of fabric for the back, 12 x 5 inches (30.5 x 12.7 cm)

✖ 1 ½ cups of rice

✖ Bowl

✖ 15 drops lavender essential oil

Instructions

1. Determine the order of the three fabric pieces for the front of the eye pillow, and place them together along the 4-inch (10.16-cm) sides. Pin two together, right sides facing, and sew together along one 4-inch side.

2. Pin the third fabric piece in place, right sides facing, and sew together along one 4-inch side. Iron all seams open.

3. Place the front piece on top of the back piece, matching the edges and sides with the right sides facing. Pin the two pieces together (figure A).

A

4. Sew all the way around the piece, leaving a 2-inch (5.08 cm) opening on each of the shorter sides. Turn the piece right-side out and iron.

5. Push seams in on one open side and iron. Sew down the length of that entire side.

6. Place the rice in a bowl and add the lavender essential oil drops. Stir together.

7. Pour rice into opening on the open side of the pillow, then push in seams and iron. Make sure the rice is pushed to the closed side while you sew to avoid a mess. Sew down the length of that side to close.

NOTE: *All seam allowances are ¼ inch (6 mm) unless otherwise specified.*

MODERN NURSING BAG

DESIGNER ✖ JESSICA FEDIW

Stylish and discreet, this is the perfect nursing bag. The interior features a variety of pockets for storage of bottles and breast pump accessories. Vinyl lining throughout the interior and a vinyl, faux-leather material on the bottom of the bag allow for quick and easy cleanup of any spills.

MATERIALS & TOOLS

✖ Canvas fabric, 1 yard (.9 m)

✖ Leather-like vinyl, ½ yard (.46 m)

✖ Lightweight vinyl, 1 yard (.91 m)

✖ Medium-weight interfacing, 1 yard (.91 m)

✖ Scissors

✖ Pins

✖ Sewing machine and supplies

✖ Heavyweight metal separating zipper, 20 inches or 22 inches (50.8 cm or 55.9 cm)

✖ 2 Fashion D-rings, 1 inch (2.5 cm) each

✖ 2 Fashion swivel hooks

✖ Ruler or flexible measuring tape

Instructions

1. Cut the following pieces:

FOR THE BAG'S EXTERIOR:

- 2 canvas fabric pieces, each 20 x 12 inches (50.8 x 30.5 cm)

- 2 pieces leather-like vinyl, each 20 x 8.5 inches (50.8 x 21.6 cm)

FOR THE BAG'S INTERIOR:

- 2 pieces lightweight vinyl, each 20 x 19.5 inches (50.8 x 49.5 cm)

- 2 pieces lightweight vinyl, each 20 x 14 inches (50.8 x 35.6 cm)

- 2 pieces medium-weight interfacing, each 20 x 19.5 inches (50.8 x 49.5 cm)

FOR THE STRAP:

- 1 piece leather-like vinyl, 3 x 40.5 inches (7.6 x 102.9 cm)

- 4 pieces leather-like vinyl, each 1 inch x 5 inches (2.5 x 12.7 cm)

2. Take one of the canvas fabric pieces and lay it down, right-side up. Place one of the 20-inch (50.8 cm) leather-like vinyl pieces on top, right-side down, matching up along the 20-inch (50.8 cm) edges. Sew together and then lightly iron the seam open. Repeat with the other two pieces (figure A).

A

3. Place the two exterior pieces together with right sides facing, and match up the seams. Sew down one side, across the bottom, and up the other side, leaving the top open (the canvas edge) (figure B).

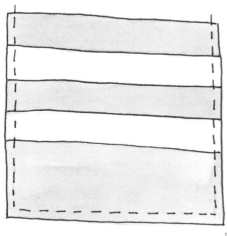

B

4. Push one bottom corner out and flatten to create a triangle. The side seam and the bottom seam need to match up (figure C). Measure 3 inches (7.6 cm) from the edge of the fabric in toward the center (figure D). Use a pin to mark this area. Sew across at the 3-inch (7.6 cm) mark, and cut off the excess fabric at the seam (figure E). Repeat on the other side. Turn right-side out, and push the new, squared corners out.

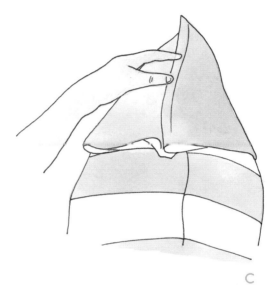

C

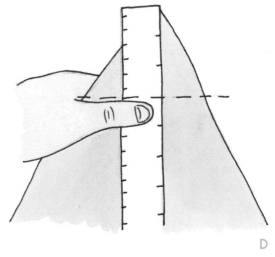

D

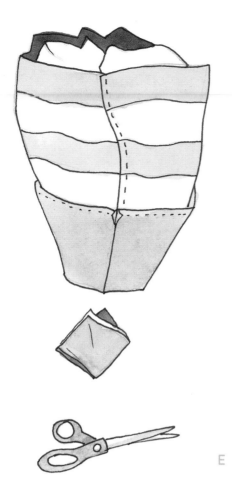

7. Lay down a piece of the medium-weight interfacing. Place one of the 20 x 19.5-inch (50.8 x 49.5-cm) lightweight vinyl pieces on top with the right side facing up. Pin the pocket piece on so the top of the pocket is 5 inches (12.7 cm) from the top. Sew the sides and bottom of the pocket in place. Repeat with the other pieces.

8. Sew two lines down each pocket, each 6 inches (15.3 cm) in from the left and right sides. This creates the pocket partitions.

9. Place the two interior pieces together, right sides facing, and match up the pockets (this is the bottom of the bag). Sew down the side, across the bottom, and up the other side.

10. With the wrong side facing out, push one corner out and flatten to create a triangle. The side seam and the bottom seam need to match up. Measure 3 inches (7.6-cm) from the edge of the fabric in toward the center. Use a pin to mark this area. Sew across at the 3-inch (7.6-cm) mark and cut off excess fabric at the seam. Repeat for the other side. Leave the wrong side turned out (figure F).

11. Place the interior piece inside the exterior piece. Line up the side seams and pin together. Fold the top down about ¼ inch (6 mm) and press. Fold down again about ¼ inch (6 mm) and press. Topstitch around the entire top of the bag (figure G).

For the bag's interior:

5. Fold each of the 20 x 14-inch (50.8 x 35.6-cm) pieces of lightweight vinyl in half on the 14-inch (35.6-cm) length, right sides facing. Sew along the 20-inch (50.8-cm) edge to create a tube. Turn right-side out and flatten the seam with your fingers. You've just created the interior pocket pieces.

6. With the right-side facing, sew along the edge on one 20-inch (50.8-cm) side of the interior pocket piece. Repeat with the other interior pocket piece.

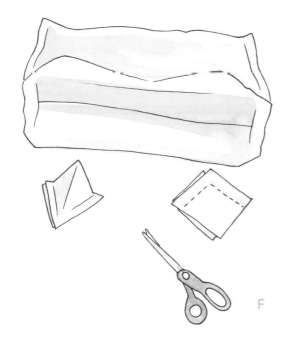

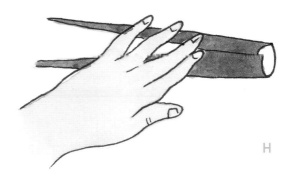

For the strap:

12. Using the 3 x 40.5-inch (7.6 x 102.9-cm) leather-like vinyl piece, fold each side to the middle of the 3-inch (7.6-cm) width (figure H). Then fold that in half and pin in place so the raw edges are hidden in the fold. Sew down the open side. Loop one end of the strap through

the fashion swivel hook and fold over 1 inch (2.5 cm). Sew in place at the end and then again, closer to the swivel hook. Repeat with the other side (figure I).

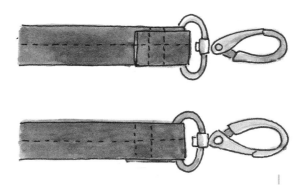

13. Make the side holders for the D-rings by placing two of the 1 x 5-inch (2.5 x 12.7-cm) leather-like vinyl pieces on top of each other, wrong sides facing. Sew down each long side. Repeat for the other two.

14. Loop one of the side holders through the D-ring and match the ends. Sew together slightly below the D-ring. Repeat for the other side holder and D-ring piece (figure J).

J

Installing the zipper:

16. Fold down the fabric end of the zipper on one side. Pin that top zipper side onto one of the inner edges of the purse top. Line up the top of the zipper to 1 inch (2.5 cm) before the side seam. Note that the other end of the zipper will be longer than the purse side. Sew zipper in place, stopping 1 inch (2.5 cm) before the seam where the end of the zipper is (figure L).

15. Take one D-ring with holder and place on the side seam of the bag. Its middle should line up on the seam, and the top of the D-ring will need to be 4 inches (10.2 cm) from the top of the bag. Sew it in place at the bottom of the holder and also a little above it, as close to the D-ring as possible. Repeat with the other side (figure K).

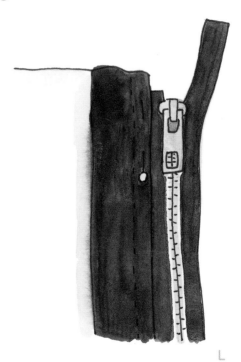

L

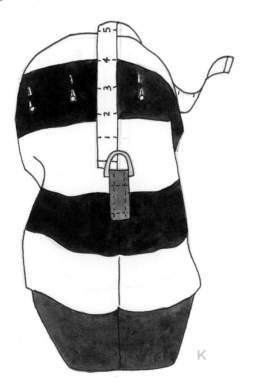

K

17. Unzip the zipper and fold down the fabric end of the zipper on the other side. Pin this side to the inner edge of the purse on the other side (just as before) and sew in place. Zip the zipper halfway shut. Push the leftover zipper end down into the purse.

18. Hook the strap onto the D-rings.

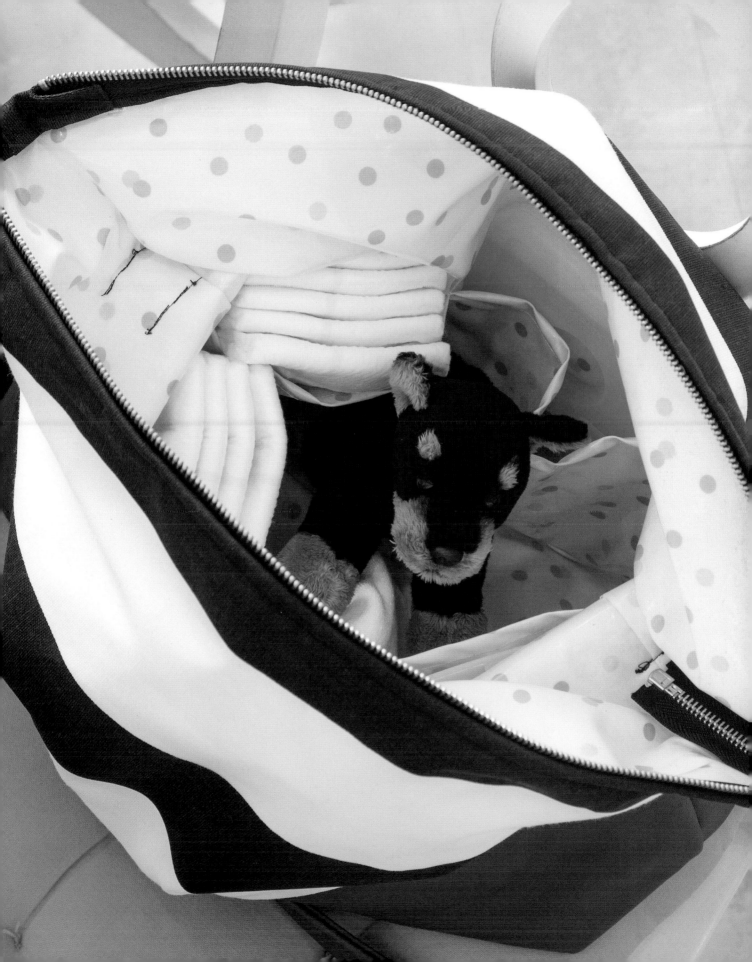

LIGHTWEIGHT NURSING INFINITY SCARF

DESIGNER ✕ JESSICA FEDIW

Create a quick and easy nursing cover that doubles as a stylish infinity scarf when not in use. Gauze fabric is a nice lightweight and breathable material, but other fabrics, such as knits, can be used to create a warmer scarf.

MATERIALS & TOOLS

- 2 yards (1.8 m) gauze fabric
- Pins
- Sewing machine and supplies
- Scissors
- Iron

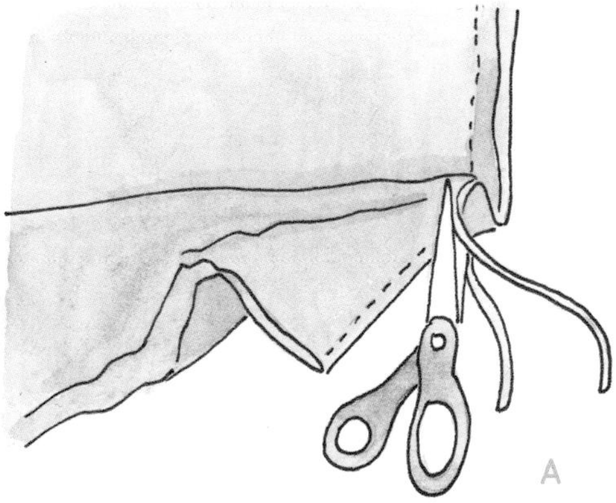

A

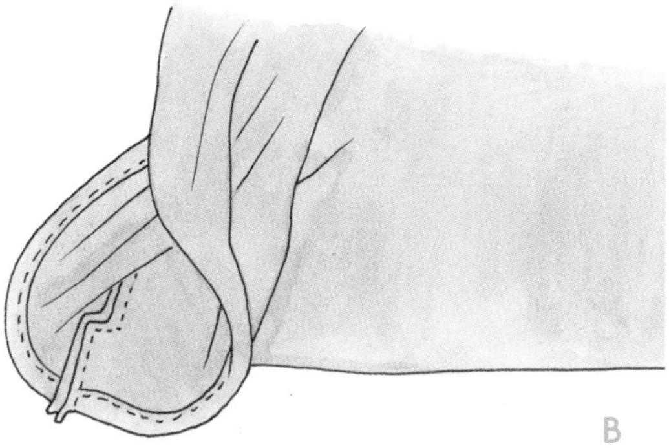

B

Instructions

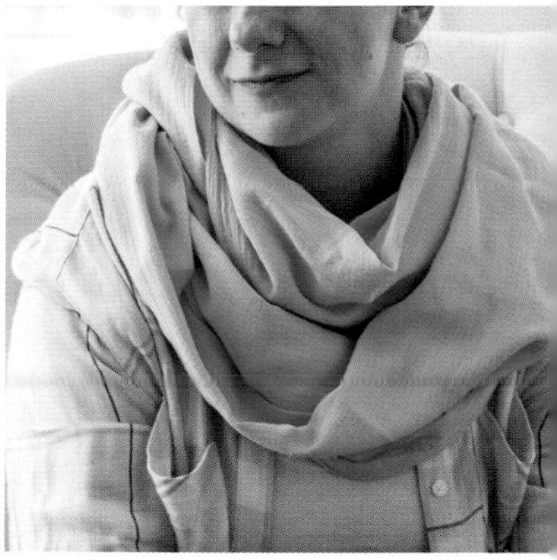

1. Fold the 2 yards of gauze fabric in half width-wise along the full length of fabric, right sides facing. Pin along the long, open side and sew together to make a tube.

2. Turn the fabric right-side out. Place the two open ends of the tube together, making sure the side seams match up. Pin and sew together.

3. Trim the seam allowance as close as possible. Take care not to cut the thread (figure A).

4. Pushing the rest of the tube of fabric out of the way, open up and flatten out the fabric along the seam. Fold the fabric back onto itself along the seam (the raw edge should now be covered inside). Press the entire length of the seam flat at the fold. Sew a small seam allowance along the length (figure B).

NOTE: *All seam allowances are ¼ inch (6 mm) unless otherwise specified.*

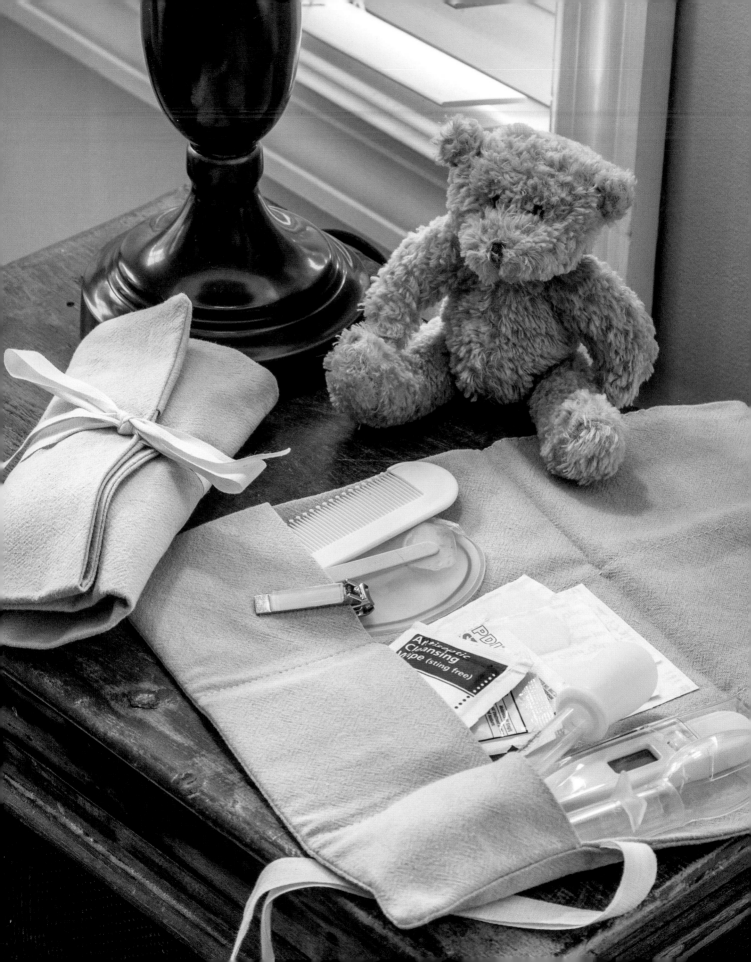

FOLD-UP FIRST AID KIT

DESIGNER ✕ VALERIE LLOYD

This simple sewing project makes a pretty and practical organizer for essential first-aid items. The pockets are roomy enough to hold a variety of bandages, ointment packets, and small tools. It folds up into a compact pouch—perfect for tucking into a purse or diaper bag—and closes with cotton ribbon ties. Only a small amount of cloth is needed, so it's a good opportunity to use fabric scraps or old flour sack dishtowels.

MATERIALS & TOOLS

- 12 inches (30.5 cm) fabric at least 30 inches (76.2 cm) wide
- Scissors
- Iron
- Sewing pins
- Ruler or flexible measuring tape
- Erasable fabric pen, pencil, or chalk
- Sewing machine
- Thread
- 1 yard (.9 m) cotton ribbon

Instructions

1. Cut out a piece of fabric measuring 9½ x 6 inches (24.1 x 15.2 cm). Fold it in half lengthwise, and press with an iron. This will be the interior pocket.

2. Cut out two pieces of fabric measuring 9½ x 11½ inches (24.1 x 29.2 cm). Lay the pocket on the lower edge of one of the fabric pieces, matching up the sides and raw edges. Pin in place (figure A). Use a ruler or flexible measuring tape and an erasable fabric pen, pencil, or chalk to mark two vertical lines—one 3¾ inches (9.5 cm) from the left side and one 2¾ inches (7 cm) from the right side (figure B). Sew along the two vertical lengths, following the line you marked (figure C). This will create three pockets, though one will be slightly larger to accommodate bandages and larger items.

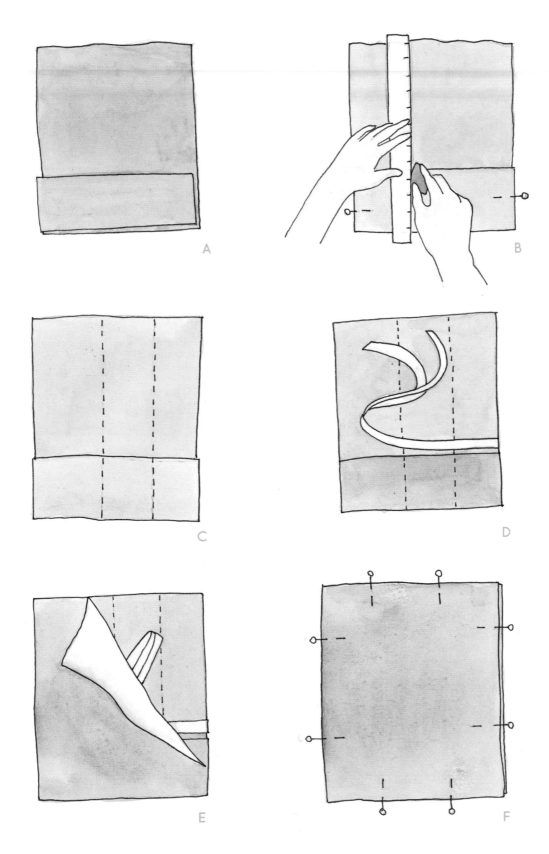

3. Fold the length of cotton ribbon in half and place the folded end on the right-side edge of the fabric, just above the pocket. The rest of the ribbon should be folded flat on top of the fabric so that it does not get caught in the seams when they are sewn (figure D). Lay the other 9½ x 11½-inch (24.1 x 29.2-cm) piece of fabric facedown over the top (figure E). Pin all around the edges, making sure to pin the folded edge of the ribbon in place (figure F).

4. Sew around the entire edge with a ⅜-inch (9.5-mm) seam allowance, leaving a small section open near the top to allow for turning right-side out. Snip off the corners, turn right-side out, and press. Hand-sew the opening closed with Running Stitch, or machine-sew with Zigzag Stitch.

5. Fold the top down to the pockets, and press the top edge. To close the pouch, fold the sides in, wrap the ribbon around, and tie a bow. Snip the excess ribbon.

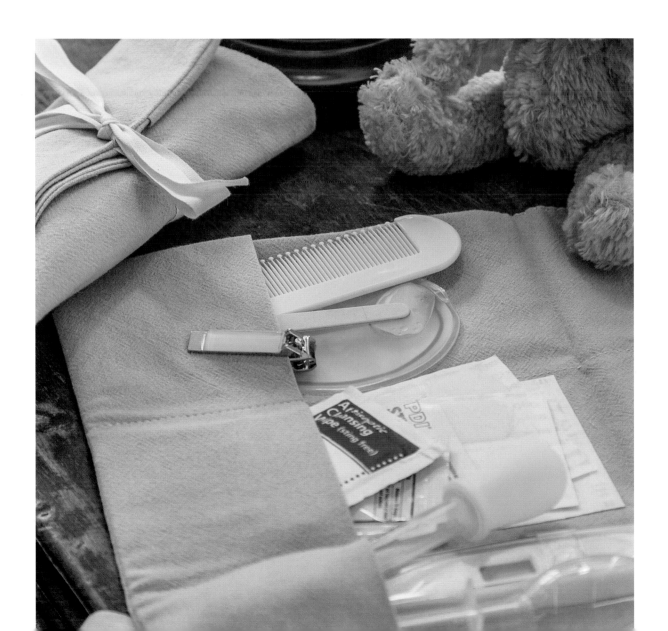

DIAPER CHANGE MAT CLUTCH

DESIGNERS ✕ TESS & RAE

MATERIALS & TOOLS

1 piece high-loft fusible fleece, 33 x 13 inches (83.8 x 33 cm)

Medium-weight or heavyweight interfacing, for flap and pocket backings

1 piece quilting cotton or other home décor fabric, 33 x 13 inches (83.8 x 33 cm), for exterior

1 piece quilting cotton, laminated cotton, fleece, or plush microfiber fabric for babies in contrasting color, 33 x 13 inches (83.8 x 33 cm), for interior

1 piece 3/4-inch (2-cm) wide hook-and-loop tape, 1 1/2 inches (4 cm) long

2 fabric pieces in contrasting color, 3 x 10 inches (7.6 x 25.4 cm), for flap closure

4 fabric pieces, 7 x 12 inches (17.8 x 30.5 cm), for 2 pockets' backings

2 fabric pieces, 7 x 10 inches (17.8 x 25.4 cm), for pockets

Erasable fabric pen, pencil, or chalk

Pins

Iron

This Diaper Change Mat Clutch is the perfect item for busy, on-the-go moms. Its compact design means it's both easy to carry and big enough to serve as a surface for quick diaper changes. Fill the pockets with a few diapers, a packet of wipes, and a disposable changing mat cover, and you're all set!

Instructions

1. Lay the fusible fleece adhesive-side up on an ironing surface. Lay the exterior fabric right-side up atop the fusible fleece. Iron these two layers together.

2. Cut the interfacing into pieces to match the size of the two flap-closure pieces and the four pocket-backing pieces. Iron the interfacing to each of the pieces.

3. Sew the hook side of the hook-and-loop tape to the outside body of the mat according to the diagram (pages 46-47). See figure A.

4. Sew the soft loop side of the hook-and-loop tape to the right side of one of the flap-closure pieces, approximately ¾ inch (2 cm) from lower edge, making sure it is centered side to side (figure A.)

5. For the closure flap: Place the flap pieces right sides together. Sew around the pieces using a ¼-inch (6 mm) seam allowance. Leave a gap approximately 1½ inches (3.8 cm) along one long side of the flap in the center. Turn the flap piece right-side out, and make sure all four corners are neatly squared off. Iron and Edgestitch around the entire flap, ensuring that the gap has been closed during stitching. Attach the flap to the outside body of the mat (figure B). Pin the flap in place, making sure the hook-and-loop tape side is facing down.

Use an erasable fabric pen, pencil, or chalk to mark a rectangle on the top edge of the flap approximately ¾ inch (2 cm) in width. Sew around the rectangle. Mark an X shape through the rectangle and sew along the lines to securely attach the flap closure to the body of the mat (figure B).

6. For the pockets: Fold one of the short edges over by ½ inch (1.3 cm) on each pocket piece, then fold over again and sew in place. Place the two pocket backings right sides

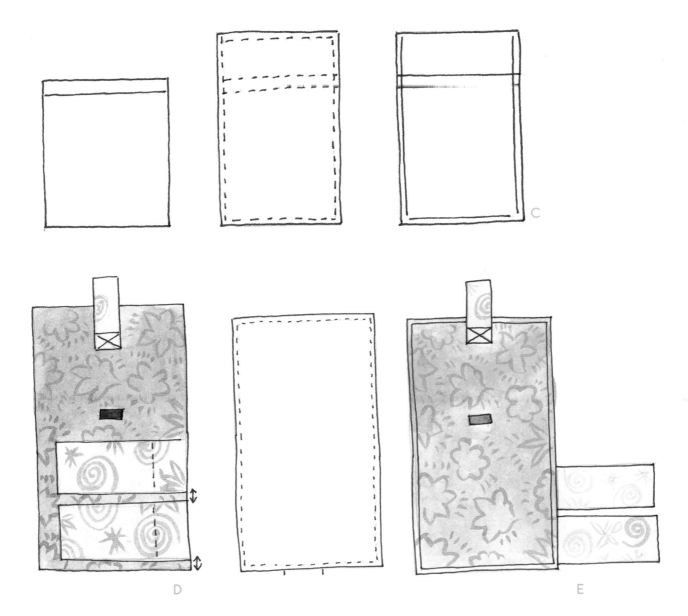

together with the pocket piece in the middle. Line up the pocket piece along the bottom edge. Sew around the bottom and two sides using a ½-inch (1.3 cm) seam allowance, leaving the top edge open. Turn right-side out and press. Topstitch all the way around (figure C).

7. Attach the two pocket pieces to the outside body of the mat (figure D). Pin the pockets in place with the front of the pocket pieces facing downward so that they are on top of the outside of the mat. Be sure that the closure flap is also folded inward on top of the body of the mat.

8. Position the inside body of the mat facedown on top of the outside body of the mat so that the right sides are together. Sew around all four sides, using a ½-inch (2.5-cm) seam allowance and leaving a 6-inch (15.2 cm) gap

open on the lower edge of mat. Turn the mat right-side out and press, ensuring that the pocket pieces and the closure flap are in place. Edgestitch around the mat, making sure the gap has been closed during stitching (figure E).

9. To use the Diaper Change Mat Clutch, fold the pockets inward onto the mat, and starting at the bottom, fold the clutch three times to engage the hook-and-loop flap closure (figure F).

F

MATERNITY PILLOW

DESIGNER �֍ EMILIE AKKERMANS

Rest well with the help of a personalized maternity pillow. It can be hard to find a store-bought maternity pillow that suits all of a new mom's needs—is it big enough? Does the filling offer enough comfort and support? Is the fabric soft? By making your own, you ensure the pillow will suit your own individual preferences.

MATERIALS & TOOLS

�֍ Templates 1-10 (pages 118-127)

✖ 10 sheets of paper, each 7 x 9 inches (18 x 23 cm)

✖ Tape

✖ Scissors

✖ Pen or pencil

✖ Thin tracing paper or tissue paper

✖ Fabric of your choice (see Note, next page)

✖ Straight pins

✖ Sewing machine and thread

✖ Polyester stuffing, about 11 pounds (5 kg)

✖ Needle

Instructions

1. You will need 10 sheets of paper that are 7 x 9 inches (18 x 23 cm). If your copy paper is larger than 7 x 9 inches (18 x 23 cm), then trim the pages to size. Copy each template onto its own sheet of paper, taking care to label each one with the correct number. Beginning with Template 1 at the top left, lay out Templates 1 through 4 on the top row, Templates 5 through 8 on the second row, and Templates 9 and 10 on the third row (figure A). A larger version of the below diagram is available on page 117.

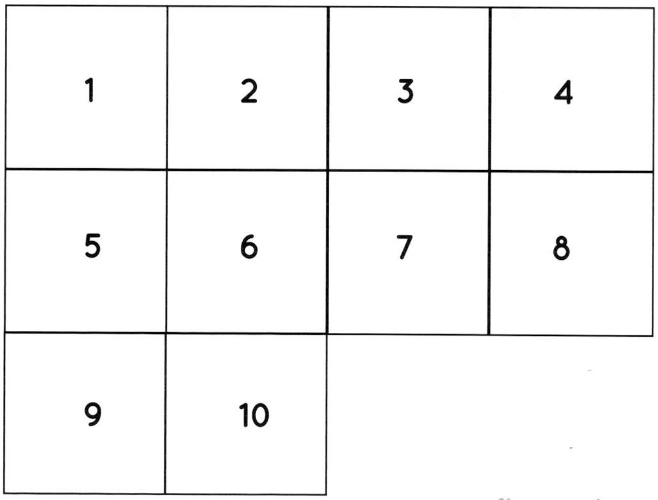

1	2	3	4
5	6	7	8
9	10		

figure A

2. Adjust the templates slightly until all the papers' straight edges meet and the template line is continuous, without any gaps. The template lines should just barely touch each other, not overlapping more than a few centimeters. Tape the papers together, and cut out the pattern. This is half of the pillow template.

3. Tape together enough thin tracing paper or tissue paper to fit the pattern, or use old newspaper (just be mindful about the ink rubbing off on your fabric). Trace the pattern onto your paper of choice, then cut it out—this is the second half of your maternity pillow pattern. Tape the two pattern pieces together on the straight ends, making sure the curves both face the same direction to form a very large C-shape. Your template is ready to use!

4. On a large, flat surface, lay out the fabric of your choice in a single layer. Fold the fabric in half, right sides together. If you are using narrow (or 44-inch [112-cm]) fabric, fold the shorter sides together. If you are using wide (or 60-inch [152-cm]) fabric, fold the longer sides

together. Using straight pins, pin the pattern to the fabric. Place the pins parallel to the black line of the pattern, and include the pattern and both layers of fabric when you pin. Cut out the pattern. Remove the pins and the pattern.

5. Leaving fabrics right sides together, pin again, but this time place the pins perpendicular to the fabric's edges, with the head of the pin slightly off the edges. Beginning on the inside curve of the pattern and using a ½ inch (1.3 cm) seam allowance, sew around the whole pillow, leaving a large opening for stuffing on the inside curve. Reinforce the tight inner curves with several lines of stiches. Clip the curves and finish the seam allowance edge with a Zigzag Stitch.

6. Turn the pillow right-side out. It's time to stuff your pillow! Test the firmness of your pillow as you stuff it, and adjust the amount of stuffing to suit your desired comfort level. When stuffing, grab big pieces of polyester filling from the package; inserting small clumps results in a lumpy look. Begin by filling the furthest end of the pillow, then stuff the closest end, and finish with where your opening is. If you see any lumps in the stuffing, just place your hand inside the pillow to massage the stuffing and break up the lump.

7. Hand-stich the opening closed.

MATERNITY SKIRT

DESIGNER ✖ EMILIE AKKERMANS

Make this comfy, stylish maternity maxi skirt to wear during uncomfortably hot summer days. The bottom portion of the skirt is made using a fabric of your choice, and the stretchy top portion will comfortably cover any expecting mom's bump. Make a few of these in a variety of your favorite patterned cotton fabrics; they'll be staples in your summer wardrobe.

MATERIALS, TOOLS, AND SUPPLIES

✖ Flexible measuring tape

✖ Pen or pencil and paper, for writing down your measurements

✖ 2 large pieces of thin tracing paper or tissue paper

✖ Stretch fabric, 12 inches (30.5 cm)

✖ Fabric of your choice for skirt, 2 yards (1.8 meters)

✖ Pins

✖ Scissors

✖ Matching thread

✖ Sewing machine with rounded-tip needle (for stretch fabric)

✖ Iron

✖ Erasable fabric pen, pencil, or chalk

Instructions

1. With flexible measuring tape, record the approximate distance from your waist to your hip. Write this measurement down and label it A. Loosely measure the distance around your waist and add 1 inch (2.5 cm) to the number. Record this measurement and label it B. Loosely measure the distance around your hips and add 1 inch (2.5 cm). Record this measurement and label it C.

2. On the first large piece of thin tracing paper or tissue paper and using your labeled measurements, draw a rectangle the length of A high and ½ the length of B wide.

3. Fold your stretch fabric in half. Place pattern on the fold, making sure the fabric is positioned so that the stretch runs along the longer B side of your pattern (figure A). Pin and cut.

4. Fold the edge of the stretch fabric over ½ inch (1.3 cm) and press. Using a sewing machine fitted with a rounded-tip sewing machine needle, sew a Zigzag Stitch ⅛ inch (2.3 mm) in from the fold.

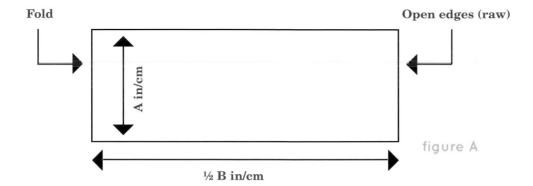

Fold   **Open edges (raw)**

A in/cm

½ B in/cm

5. Fold the stretch fabric piece in half, right sides together, and sew along the shorter side with a Zigzag Stitch to create a tube. Starting at the seam, measure and mark the tube into 4 equal sections with the erasable fabric pen, pencil, or chalk. First, mark directly opposite of the seam at the top, hemmed side of the stretch fabric. Using the seam and first mark as a reference, draw the second and third marks at the quarter and three-quarter spots (if this is confusing, think of the quarter-hours on a clock face, envisioning the back seam as 12:00). Also mark the bottom edge of the stretch fabric at the second and third marks. Set aside.

6. Using your flexible measuring tape, determine the length of your skirt by measuring from your hip to where you want the bottom of the skirt to be and add 2 inches (5 cm). Label this number D.

7. On the edge of the second piece of large paper, place a mark near the top and label it E. Starting at E, draw a line ¼ of your hip measurement (C) perpendicular to the edge of the paper. Label this line F. On the edge of the paper, measure along line F the length of D, starting from point E. Label this point H. Draw a straight line the length of D starting from F at an angle. Label this angled line G. You can make this angle sharper or wider depending on how wide you want the bottom of your skirt to be (figure B).

8. Draw a slightly curved line between D and G. This is your bottom hemline (figure B).

9. Fold the skirt fabric in half lengthwise. Place the pattern on top, making sure that the line from E to H aligns on the fold. Pin and cut out. Repeat this step. You should have two identical pieces; one will be the front of your skirt and the other the back. Using an erasable fabric pen, pencil, or chalk, mark the top of each piece at its center. Make sure you've aligned the top and bottom correctly. With right sides together and using ½ inch (2.5 cm) seam allowance, sew the front to the back at the side seams with a Running Stitch.

10. Notice that the bottom, raw circumference of the stretch fabric is shorter than the circumference of the top edge of the skirt. With right sides together for both pieces, slip the stretchy fabric over the skirt so that the

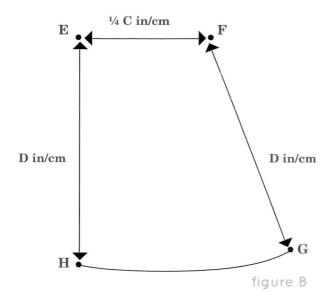

¼ C in/cm

E

F

D in/cm

D in/cm

H

G

figure B

Template measurements:

E to F = ¼ of C (hipline)

E to H = length of skirt;
center front and back

F to G = side of skirt

(E to H and F to G should be the
same length)

H to G = hemline

bottom, raw edge of the stretch fabric is lined up with the top, raw edge of the skirt. Align the marks you made on the stretch fabric to the sides and center of the skirt fabric. Pin the two fabrics together at these four points, making sure the stretch fabric has been evenly pulled to match the circumference of the skirt.

11. Continue pinning around the edge until you have enough pins in place to make it easier to machine sew and the stretchy fabric is evenly distributed. It's okay if the two pieces don't line up perfectly—you will adjust the stretch fabric as it goes through the sewing machine so it lines up with the skirt piece.

12. Sew with a Zigzag Stitch all around. Start where there is one pin, put the sewing machine foot down to hold the fabric in place, and remove the pin. Hold the next pin, and stretch the fabric until it lines up with the skirt piece. Sew along the edge, keeping this tension. Once you get to the next pin, remove it and repeat.

13. Hem the bottom, raw edge of the skirt by folding it over ½ inch (1.3 cm) twice and pressing. Sew along this folded edge with Running Stitch.

RAINBOW BABY SLING

DESIGNER ✖ MOLLIE JOHANSON

Hold baby close in this hand-embroidered ring sling. The colorful design of the tail will keep your little one entertained, and you'll have your hands free!

MATERIALS & TOOLS

✖ Linen, 2 ½ yards (2.3 m)

✖ Scissors

✖ Iron

✖ Thread

✖ Sewing machine

✖ Pins

✖ Accent fabric, 25 x 3 inches (63.5 cm x 7.6 cm) or 1 yard (0.9m) double-fold bias tape

✖ 2 aluminum rings, each 3 inches (7.6 cm)

✖ Embroidery design (page 129)

✖ Water-soluble pen or other embroidery transfer method

✖ Embroidery needle

✖ Embroidery floss: 1 skein each in coral, yellow, medium-orange spice, avocado green, moss green, dark-teal green, light-teal green, medium-blue violet, dark-cornflower blue, ultra-dark dusty rose, and black

 NOTE: *If you prefer a longer tail or want to allow more room as your little one grows, consider using 3 yards (2.7 meters) of linen.*

 TIP: *For safety, only use rings designed for baby slings.*

Instructions

1. Holding two diagonally opposite corners of the linen fabric, gently pull the fabric, stretching it as far as possible. Switch to holding the other two corners and pull again. This is most easily done with the help of another person. This will straighten the weave of the fabric, ensuring straight, even edges along the cut of lines. If the fabric does not square up with the first pullings, repeat a second time.

2. Cut the linen fabric into a rectangle that is 26 inches (66 cm) wide and 2½ yards (2.3 meters) long.

3. Hem the sides. Fold and press the long edges in ½ inch (1.3 cm), then fold and press them in ½ inch (1.3 cm) again. Sew the folded hem ⅛ inch (3.2 mm) in from the inside fold.

4. Attach the accent fabric. Fold and press the accent fabric piece in half the long way and press each of the long edges in ⅜ inch (.95 cm). Press each end in ½ inch (1.3 cm) or the amount needed to make the strip match the width of the hemmed linen. Pin the right side of the fabric strip to the back of the linen, with raw edges aligned. Sew along the closest pressed crease. Fold the strip around to the front side of the linen, wrapping the raw edge inside, and Topstitch the two short sides and along the top folded edge of the accent fabric.

5. To attach the aluminum rings: Zigzag Stitch about ¼ inch (.6 cm) wide along the entire length of the linen's raw edge to keep it from the fraying. Add a line of Running Stitches on each side. On the right side of the fabric, mark across the width of the fabric at 16 inches (40.6 cm) from the zigzagged edge. Slide the end of the fabric through the two rings and align it along the marked line, right sides together. Baste the end in place by hand. Sew three lines of Running Stitches along the zigzagged edge, ¼ inch (6 mm) apart. Backstitch each end. Remove the Basting Stitches.

6. Transfer the embroidery design (page 129) onto the right side of the sling, several inches above the accent fabric (for instructions on transferring, see page 13). Take care to center it. Embroider the hexagon design with three strands of embroidery floss using Backstitch. Embroider the faces with three strands of black embroidery floss. Make the eyes with French Knots and the mouths with Backstitch. Remove any transfer markings.

7. To wear the sling, slide the embroidered tail through both rings, then fold it back over the first ring and through the second ring. With the tail of the sling toward the front, place your arm through the middle and bring the sling over your head. Keep the rings to the front and close to your shoulder. Place your baby in the sling, and pull the tail to tighten and secure it.

> ❋ NOTE: *The folded hem may show on the outside of the main part of the sling, but it should be hidden by the embroidered tail.*

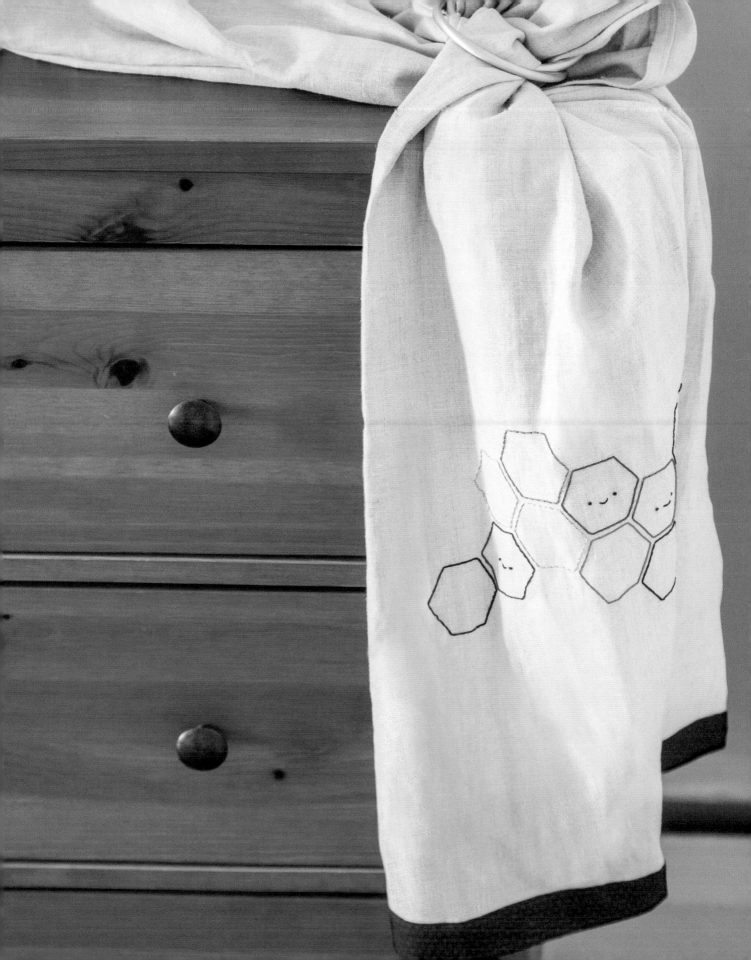

BABY

TUMMY TIME FLOOR QUILT

DESIGNER ✖ MOLLIE JOHANSON

Strengthen and stretch baby's muscles with some tummy time on this small quilt with high-contrast patchwork and a happy heart.

MATERIALS & TOOLS

- ✖ 2 bundles fat eighth quilting cotton in red and light yellow, for heart block

- ✖ Fabric scissors

- ✖ Rotary cutter

- ✖ Mat

- ✖ Erasable fabric pen, pencil, or chalk

- ✖ Sewing machine and thread

- ✖ Iron

- ✖ Embroidery design (page 129)

- ✖ Embroidery hoop

- ✖ Embroidery needle

- ✖ Embroidery floss: 1 skein in black

- ✖ 2 pieces black printed quilting cotton, each ¼ yard (.23 m), for strips

- ✖ 2 pieces white printed quilting cotton, each ¼ yard (.23 m), for strips

- ✖ 1 piece quilting cotton, 1¼ yard (1.1 m), for backing

- ✖ 1 piece batting, 44 x 44 inches (112 x 112 cm)

- ✖ Pins

- ✖ Safety pins

- ✖ Masking tape

- ✖ 1 piece quilting cotton, ³⁄₈ yard (.34 m), for binding

- ✖ Black no. 8 perle cotton

- ✖ Needle

> ✖ **NOTE:** *Use ¼-inch (6-mm) seam allowance throughout. Wash fabrics before starting this project.*

> ✖ **TIP:** *A "fat eighth" is a cut of fabric particular to quilting and is handy for when you need a small amount of fabric.*

Instructions

1. FOR THE HEART BLOCK: Using either the fabric scissors or a rotary cutter and mat, cut two 6-inch (15.2-cm) squares, one each from the red and light-yellow quilting cotton. Cut two 3½-inch (8.9-cm) squares, one each from the red and light-yellow quilting cotton. Finally, cut one 3 x 10½-inch (7.6 x 26.7-cm) rectangle from the red quilting cotton.

2. SEW HALF-SQUARE TRIANGLES (HSTs): Place the larger red and light-yellow squares with right sides together, and mark a line diagonally across the wrong side of the yellow square from point to point with an erasable fabric pen, pencil, or chalk. Sew ¼ inch (6 mm) from each side of the marked line. Cut on the center line and press the seams open. Repeat with the smaller squares.

3. SEW THE HEART BLOCK TOGETHER: Join the two large HSTs together with red sides touching so that they form the bottom point of the heart. Repeat with the smaller HSTs to make two points, then sew those two points together with light-yellow sides touching to make the top of the heart. Sew the heart top to the top of the long rectangle and the heart bottom to the bottom of the long rectangle. Press all seams open.

4. EMBROIDER THE HEART FACE: Trace the embroidery pattern onto the rectangle section of the heart. Use six strands of black floss. Using the embroidery hoop, embroider the eyes with Satin Stitch and the mouth with Backstitch.

5. Using either the scissors or rotary cutter and mat, cut fifteen 3 x 10½-inch (7.6 x 26.7 cm) rectangles from each of the black-printed and white-printed fabrics.

> ❋ TIP: *If your fabrics are directional, some of the strips will have the print turned. You can mix in these turned strips or buy a larger cut of fabric to avoid this.*

6. Sew strips together by alternating the black and the white rectangles and sewing the long edges together. Form three large pieces, each with sixteen rectangles. For the piece with the heart block, start by sewing three alternating rectangles, followed by the heart block, and then nine alternating rectangles. Press the seams on the wrong side. Join the four pieces

NOTE: *You can place the heart block anywhere on the quilt or add more than one!*

together, pinning and sewing so that the corners of each of the rectangles match up. Press the seams open.

7. To Baste the quilt, make a quilt sandwich by laying the backing fabric on a large, flat surface, wrong side up. Secure the fabric to the floor with tape, making sure that it is as smooth and even as possible. Lay the batting on top, then place the quilt top onto the batting with the right side up. Pin the layers together with safety pins. Place a pin in every other rectangle.

8. Quilt the blanket by using your favorite quilting method or sewing soft wavy lines horizontally across the quilt. Trim the edges so the quilt is square.

9. Cut five 2½-inch (6.4-cm) strips of binding fabric. Join the strips by placing the ends of two strips right sides together and perpendicular to each other. Sew a diagonal line across the overlap (not from the inner angle to the outer point). Join all strips, and press the seams open. Fold and press one end under ½ inch (1.3 cm). Fold and press the strip in half lengthwise to make a binding piece that is 1¼ inches (3.2 cm) wide. For a reminder on binding techniques, turn to page 11.

10. SEW THE BINDING TO THE QUILT: Starting in the middle of one side with the folded-under end and placing right sides together, lay the raw edge of the binding strip along the edge on the backside of the quilt. Pin the folded edge of the binding to the quilt to hold it in place. Begin stitching 1 inch (2.5 cm) from the pin, leaving the first inch free. Sew a seam ⅝ inch (1.6 cm) from the edge, stopping within ¼ inch (6 mm) of the first corner, then Backstitch and cut off the thread. Fold the strip to the outside at a 90-degree angle and then back over so that it is aligned with the next side of the quilt. Continue sewing the binding until you are within 6 inches (15.2 cm) of the start of the binding. Trim the binding so there is roughly 1 inch (2.5 cm) of overlap, and then place the cut end inside the fold of the starting end. Finish sewing.

11. To turn the binding onto the face of the quilt, fold the portion of the binding strip that extends beyond the edge of the quilt back onto itself, butting the raw edge of the binding against the edge of the quilt. Using the iron, press the fold lightly.

12. Thread a needle with about 36 inches (91.4 cm) of black no. 8 perle cotton, and knot the end. Bring the needle through the seam allowance on the edge of the quilt, then wrap the binding around to the front. Stitch the binding to the front with a Running Stitch that goes through the folded binding edge to the back of the quilt. The stitches should show along the inside edge of the binding on the front and right next to the binding on the back. Hide the knots under the binding as you end and begin each piece of black no. 8 perle cotton.

BABY ANIMAL BURP CLOTHS

DESIGNER ✕ MOLLIE JOHANSON

Choose from five black, white, and gray baby animals when you stitch up these darling burp cloths. The embroidered cloths add extra cuteness, while the plain version can be sewn up super quickly!

MATERIALS & TOOLS

- 1 fat quater, or 1/3 yard (.3 m) quilting cotton and 1/3 yard (.3 m) flannel
- 1 piece flannel, 1/3 yard (.3 meters)
- Embroidery designs (page 128)
- Water-soluble pen or other embroidery transfer method
- Embroidery floss: 1 skein each in black, white, and gray
- No. 8 perle cotton
- Rotary cutter, mat, and ruler (optional, but helpful)
- Pins
- Sewing machine and thread

TIP: *Wash fabrics before starting this project.*

NOTE: *Makes one burp cloth.*

Instructions

1. Cut one 10 x 20-inch (25.4 x 50.8-cm) piece from the quilting cotton and two 10 x 20-inch (25.4 x 50.8-cm) pieces from the flannel. Set the flannel aside.

2. TO EMBROIDER THE BABY ANIMAL DESIGN MOTIFS: Trace one of the baby animal embroidery designs onto the quilting cotton, taking care to center it at one end and place it about 3 inches (7.6 cm) above the bottom edge. Use four strands of floss in the colors designated by the design motifs. Secure the ends well so the stitching endures repeated washings. Use French Knots for the eyes, Satin Stitch for the nose, and Backstitch for everything else. Remove the pattern markings.

3. TO SEW THE BURP CLOTH: Keep the two flannel pieces together and treat them as one piece. Place the flannel and embroidered front right sides together and pin. Starting at the non-embroidered end, sew around the rectangle with a ¼-inch (6-mm) seam allowance, leaving a 3-inch (7.6-cm) opening. Backstitch at the beginning and end. Trim the corners and turn the cloth right-side out. Stitch the opening closed with Ladder Stitch.

4. Finish the edges. Topstitch the burp cloth ¼ inch (6 mm) from the edge with Running Stitch and the no. 8 perle cotton. If you are sewing by hand, be sure to roll the edges between your fingers to open the seams as you stitch.

TIP: *For faster burp clothes, skip the embroidery. You could also make a combination of coordinating plain and embroidered cloths as a gift.*

BITTY BEAR DIAPER BAG TAG

DESIGNER ✻ MOLLIE JOHANSON

Dress up your diaper bag and keep your little one entertained with this sweet bear tag. It's soft and squishy and can be stitched entirely by hand!

MATERIALS & TOOLS

✻ 1 piece fusible interfacing, 8 x 2½ inches (30.3 x 6.4 cm) (optional)

✻ Template and embroidery design (page 128)

✻ 1 piece of quilting cotton, 8 x 2½ inches (30.3 x 6.4 cm)

✻ Erasable fabric pen, pencil, or chalk

✻ Embroidery floss: 1 skein in dark gray

✻ 1 piece quilting cotton, 8 x 8 inches (20.3 x 20.3 cm)

✻ 1 piece felt, 8 x 8 inches (20.3 x 20.3 cm)

✻ 1 piece fusible webbing, 5 x 8 inches (12.7 x 20.3 cm)

✻ Polyester stuffing

✻ Fabric glue

✻ Hook-and-loop closure, 1¼ inch (3.2 cm)

Instructions

1. FOR THE STRAP: If you are using the fusible interfacing, iron it to the wrong side of the 8 x 2½-inch (30.3 x 6.4 cm) piece of quilting cotton. Press one end in ½ inch (1.3 cm). Press the two long edges in ¼ inch (6 mm), and then press the two folded edges in to meet in the middle. Pin the layers. Stitch where the folded edges meet on the strap. Use Running Stitch and three strands of dark-gray embroidery floss.

2. FOR THE BEAR PIECES: Lightly trace two bear templates onto the 8 x 8-inch (20.3 x 20.3-cm) piece of quilting cotton. Trace the face onto one of the shapes. Iron the quilting cotton to the felt with the fusible webbing (follow manufacturer's instructions). Cut out the shapes from the fused fabric.

3. Embroider the face using three strands of dark-gray embroidery floss. Embroider the nose and eyes with Satin Stitch, and embroider the mouth with Backstitch.

4. Sew the bear. Hold the bear shapes wrong sides together and place the strap between the ears. The side with the folded edges in the middle should be to the back, and the end with raw edges should be overlapping by at least 1 inch (2.5 cm). Pin the layers. Stitch around the bear shape with Running Stitch using three strands of dark-gray embroidery floss. Leave an opening to fill the bear with stuffing. Once the bear is stuffed, stitch the opening closed.

5. Use fabric glue to attach the two sides of the hook-and-loop closure to the back side of the strap. Place one side of the closure at the end of the strap and the other side close to the bear. Allow the glue to dry for several hours.

EMBROIDERED LINEN BIB

DESIGNER ✳ THERESA GROSH

Many families have embroidered linens (dresser scarves, tablecloths, pillow-cases, etc.) made by loved ones in previous generations. But modern tastes don't always allow for display of these heirlooms. Often, these handiworks have been marred by stains or years of neglect. The good news is, these precious items can be given new life for a new generation! This project features a baby bib cut from an embroidered linen fabric.

MATERIALS & TOOLS

✳ Template (page 110)

✳ Embroidered linen free of stains or tears in an area large enough to cut out the bib pattern, at least 9 x 12 inches (23 x 30.5 cm)

✳ Baby-soft plush microfiber fabric in coordinating color, for back of bib

✳ Erasable fabric pen, pencil, or chalk

✳ Fabric scissors

✳ Pins

✳ Thread

✳ Sewing machine (optional)

✳ 1 Snap fastener in size 15, 0.38 inch (9.7 mm)

Instructions

1. Machine-wash and -dry the embroidered linen and plush microfiber fabric. Iron the linen. The bib is a utilitarian garment—it must hold up to washing and drying.

2. Place bib template on top of the embroidered linen. Center the embroidered pattern to feature it prominently in the center of the bib. Trace lightly around the pattern with an erasable fabric pen, pencil, or chalk. Keep in mind that there will be a ¼-inch (6-mm) seam allowance.

✳ **NOTE:** *This fabric could come from any piece of embroidery and does not need to be made of linen. Examples include a scrap of tablecloth, fingertip towel, dresser scarf, etc.*

3. Cut out the bib front. Some of the embroidered pattern may get cut off. If this happens, be sure to secure any cut threads so that they don't come loose.

4. Pin bib front to plush microfiber fabric with right sides together.

5. Cut out the plush microfiber fabric, leaving at least a ½-inch (1.3-cm) border of the plush microfiber fabric beyond the edge of the bib front; plush microfiber fabric has a tendency to slide during sewing, and leaving the margin makes sewing easier (figure A).

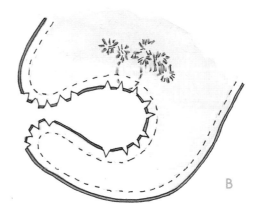

B

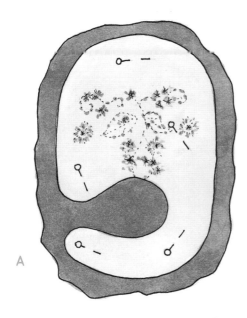

A

6. Leave a 3-inch (7.6-cm) opening at the bottom of the bib. Sew around the bib using a ¼-inch (6-mm) seam allowance.

7. Trim plush microfiber fabric all the way around so that its edge matches up with the bib front's edge.

8. Clip curves, taking care not to snip into the stitching (figure B).

9. Turn the bib right-side out through the opening.

10. Press the bib, being careful not to press directly onto the plush microfiber fabric—it will melt. Fold under the edges of the opening. Pin and press.

11. Topstitch as close to the edge as possible around the entire outside of the bib, taking care to close the opening as you go. You may want to match your top thread to the bib top and your bobbin thread to the plush microfiber fabric color.

12. Iron the bib again. Apply the snap fasteners according to the manufacturer's directions.

STRAWBERRY HAT & BOOTIES

DESIGNER ✖ CAROL SULCOSKI

I love using the color red for babies: It's gender-neutral, cheery, and looks good on all coloring. Send your tot out in style with this strawberry hat and matching booties. This knitting project is for adventurous beginners. Please refer to the Knitting section on pages 16-22 to help you get started.

FINISHED MEASUREMENTS

HAT

Sizes: Premie [Newborn, 3-6 months, 6-12 mos.]

Hat circumference: 13.5 [14.5, 16, 17] inches (36, 38, 41, 43 cm)

BOOTIES

Sizes: Premie/Newborn [3-12 months]

Cuff circumference: 4.5 [5] inches (11, 13 cm)

MATERIALS AND TOOLS

✖ 1 ball cotton blend yarn, Fine 2, in red (A), approximately 60 [80, 115, 135] yards (55, 73, 105, 123 m) **2 FINE**

✖ 1 ball cotton blend yarn, Fine 2, in leaf green (B), approximately 40 [50, 60, 75 yards] (36, 45, 55, 69 m) **2 FINE**

✖ Knitting needles: U.S. size 4 (3.5 mm) circular needle, 16-inch (40-cm) cable, or size to obtain gauge

✖ Extra circular needle or set of double-pointed needles in same size as above (for top of hat only)

✖ U.S. size 3 (3.25 mm) circular needle, or one size smaller than above (for ribbed bootie cuff only)

✖ Stitch markers

✖ Three stitch holders

✖ Tapestry needle

GAUGE

✖ 24sts/32rnds = 4-inch (10-cm) square Stockinette stitch (St st)

SPECIAL STITCH

✖ **I-CORD:** Knit across sts. Do not turn work.

* Slide sts to right-hand end of needle. Knit these same sts again, pulling working yarn snug as you knit first st. Do not turn work.

* Rep from * until cord is desired length.

HAT

Instructions

With color A, using larger circular needle, CO 82 [88, 95, 102] sts. Join for knitting in the round, being careful not to twist stitches, and place marker to show beginning of rnd.

K 16 [16, 20, 20] every rnd until hat measures 2 [2, 2.5, 2.5] inches (5, 5, 6, 6 cm)from natural roll of the brim, decr 2 [incr 2, decr 5, decr 2] sts on last rnd—80 [90, 90, 100] sts.

Begin texture pattern:

Rnd 1: *K9, p1, rep from * to end of rnd.

Rnds 2-4: K.

Rnd 5: K4, *p1, k9, rep from * to last 6 sts, p1, k5.

Rnds 6-8: K.

For 2 smallest sizes only: Continue with Leaves section at right.

For 2 largest sizes only: Rep these 8 rnds once more, then continue with Leaves section at right.

> ✿ **NOTE:** *Carry yarn loosely behind in back of work as you switch colors.*

Leaves:

Rnds 1 & 2: With color A, k4, *with color B k1, with color A k9, rep from * to last 6 sts, with color B k1, with color A k5.

Rnds 3 & 4: With color A k3, *with color B k3, with color A k7, rep from * to last 7 sts, with color B k3, with color A k4.

Rnds 5 & 6: With color A k2, *with color B k5, with color A k5, rep from * to last 8 sts, with color B k5, with color A k3.

Rnds 7 & 8: With color A k1, *with color B k7, with color A k3, rep from * to last color 9 sts, with color B k7, with color A k2.

Rnds 9 & 10: *With color B k9, with color A k1, rep from * to end of rnd. Tie off color A.

Rnds 11 & 12: With color B, knit to end.

Decrease for crown:

Rnd 13: *K8, k2tog, rep from * to end.

Rnd 14: *K7, k2tog, rep from * to end.

Rnd 15: *K6, k2tog, rep from * to end.

Continue in this fashion, knitting 1 less st before each k2tog on each rnd, until only 8 [9, 9, 10] sts remain.

Next rnd: K2tog 4 [4, 4, 5] times. Knit an additional 2ktog when making either of the two middle hat sizes—4 [5, 5, 5] sts remain.

Work I-cord Stitch on remaining sts until the "stem" measures 1.25 inches (3 cm), then cut yarn and fasten off sts.

Weave in all ends and lightly steam.

BOOTIES

> ❁ NOTE: *Booties are knit from cuff down. The top of the foot is knit, then stitches are picked up around foot to create the sides of the bootie. The booties are seamed together after the knitting is complete. Consult the diagram (page 83) for the path of knitting.*

Instructions

With color B and larger needle, CO 27 (31) sts as follows:

Using the picot cast-on method, CO 7 sts. BO first 2 sts, then slip remaining st onto left needle.

***CO** 5 more sts using the picot cast-on method, then BO first 2 sts. Slip remaining st onto left needle.

Rep from * until 25 [30] sts are on left needle, then CO 2 [1] additional st(s) – 27 [31] sts.

Working back and forth, and beginning with a k row, work in St st until the cuff measures 1.5 inches (4 cm), ending with a WS row.

Purl 2 rows (this will create the turning ridge).

Next row: With smaller needle, *k1, p1, rep from * to last st, k1.

Rep this row until ribbed portion measures 1.5 inches (4 cm), from the turning ridge. Tie off color B.

Switch to larger needle and color A, and knit 1 row.

Next row (WS): K20 [22], turn.

Next row (RS): K13 and turn.

Continue working on these 13 sts only in St st, placing first and last 7 [9] sts on separate holders, until bootie top is 1.5 [2] inches (4, 5 cm) long.

Next row (RS): K2, ssk, k to last 4 sts, k2tog, k2.

Next row (WS): P.

Rep these last 2 rows once more.

Place remaining sts on a holder.

Cut yarn.

Rejoin working yarn at the beginning of

the first red row, with RS of bootie top facing you. Knit across 7 [9] working sts remaining at beginning of row, pick up and k1 st in the gap between the ribbing and the foot top; pick up and knit 12 [14] sts alongside of the bootie top; knit across 13 sts for the bootie top including the working sts; pick up and knit 12 [14] sts down the side of the bootie top, pick up and k1 st in the gap between the foot and the ribbing; then knit rem 7 [9] working sts—53 [61] sts.

Purl 1 row.

Work 2 [4] more rows in St st.

Shape bootie:

Row 1 (RS): K20 [24], k2tog, k9, k2tog, k to end of row.

Row 2 (WS): P2, p2tog, p to last 4 sts, p2tog, p2.

Rep these 2 rows 2 [3] more times, knitting 1 less st at the beginning of the row and before the first decrease on each successive row.

BO all sts, leaving a long tail for seaming.

 NOTE: *Right-side rows will shape top of foot; wrong-side rows will shape heel.*

Finishing:

Referring to the diagram below, seam the center bottom of the bootie up to the ribbed section. Seam the ribbed section of the cuff. Mattress Stitch turnover cuff on the wrong side so the seam will be hidden when the cuff is turned over. Use light steam to block, pinning the picot edges flat.

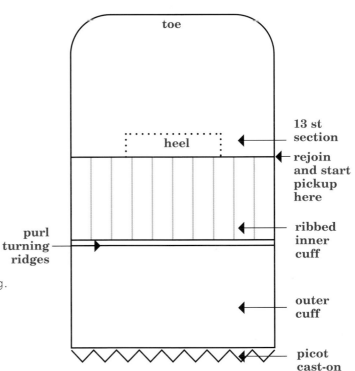

NURSERY

PLAYFUL EMBROIDERED
PENCIL HOOP ART

DESIGNER ✖ LAURA HOWARD

MATERIALS & TOOLS (TO MAKE BOTH HOOPS)

✖ Templates (page 111)

✖ 1 piece light-brown felt, 3 x 5 inches (7.6 x 12.7 cm)

✖ Felt in each of the five pencil colors, each 1 x 2½ inches (2.5 x 6.4 cm)

✖ Scissors

✖ 2 pieces white felt, each 9 x 12 inches (22.9 x 30.5 cm)

✖ 2 wooden embroidery hoops, one 6 inches (15 cm) in diameter and the other 4 inches (10 cm) in diameter

✖ Sewing thread: 1 spool each in light brown, white, and the five pencil colors

✖ Pins and sewing needle

✖ Thin tracing paper or tissue paper

✖ Baby photo

✖ Fine-tipped pen

✖ Embroidery floss: 1 skein in black

This pair of coordinating hoops would look great on a nursery wall! The large hoop, featuring baby's initials, birthdate, and picture, would also make a sweet gift for new grandparents or godparents. I chose bright, rainbow colors, but you could use rainbow pastels or shades that match your nursery décor.

Instructions

To make the large hoop:

1. Use the templates provided to cut out all the felt pieces. Cut five pieces from light-brown felt for the wooden pencil pieces and four pieces from the white felt for the photo corners. Also cut five pieces and five pencil points—one of each shape in five different colors.

2. Stretch a sheet of white felt in a 6-inch (15-cm) embroidery hoop, ensuring the felt is as tight and flat as possible. Tighten the hoop securely.

3. Arrange the five light-brown felt pieces in a row with small gaps between them. Refer to the photos for placement. Remember to leave space for the rest of the design! Pin them in place and sew them in position with matching light-brown sewing thread. Remove the pins.

4. One by one add the colored felt pieces, sewing them on top of the light-brown felt pieces with Whip Stitch and matching sewing threads.

5. Trace the outline of the baby photo template onto thin tracing paper or tissue paper. Place the template over a baby photo, then cut around it to trim the photo to size. Position the baby photo under the row of pencils and sew the four white felt pieces on one by one. Each white felt piece should stick out from the photo slightly. Use Backstitch and white sewing thread to sew flush with the edges of the photo but not through it. This way the felt creates a pocket that holds the corner of the photo in place (figure A).

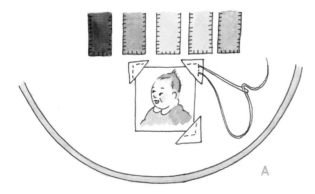

A

6. With a fine pen, write the baby's initials and birthdate on a piece of thin tracing paper or tissue paper. Use the frame provided (page 111) as a guide to ensure the writing is not too large to fit in the available space. When the ink has fully dried, cut the patterns out and pin them to either side of the photo. Use large Basting Stitches to hold the paper in place, then remove the pins.

7. Cut a piece of black embroidery floss and separate two strands. Use small Backstitches to embroider the initials and date. Then remove the Basting Stitches and carefully tear away the paper, using a pin to remove any remaining small pieces.

8. Use another two strands of black floss to sew a Running Stitch around the inside of the hoop, framing the design. Keep the stitches regular and sew flush with the edge of the hoop.

9. Trim the excess felt to about 1 inch (2.5 cm) all around the hoop. With a piece of long, double-thick white sewing thread, sew a line of Running Stitch about ¼ inch (6 mm) from the outer edge (figure B and C). Sew all the way around the edge of the felt, and then gently pull the thread, gradually pulling the felt together (figure D). When the felt is completely gathered in, secure the thread with several small stitches.

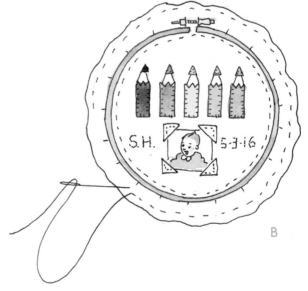

B

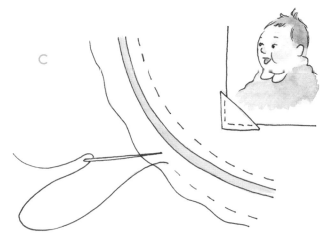

C

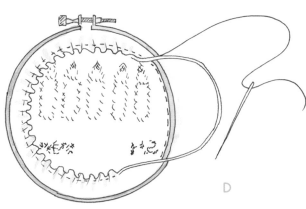

D

To make the small hoop:

1. Trace the embroidery pattern onto thin tracing paper or tissue paper with a fine pen. Allow the ink to dry completely, then trim any excess paper from around the edge of the pattern—remember to leave a border for securing the pattern to the felt in the next step.

2. Stretch a sheet of white felt in a 4-inch (10 cm) embroidery hoop, ensuring the felt is as tight and flat as possible. Tighten the hoop securely. Place the embroidery pattern in the center of the hoop, and pin it into position. Use large Basting Stitches to secure the pattern, and then remove the pins.

3. Embroider the pattern with three different shades of embroidery floss. If you're making this as part of a set with the large hoop, use coordinating colors. Split each piece of floss in two, and use half the strands (so for 6-stranded floss, use 3 strands). Backstitch along the solid lines and sew Running Stitch along the dashed lines. Use the dashes as a guide only; these do not need to be replicated exactly. Then remove the Basting Stitches, and carefully tear away the paper. Use a pin to remove any remaining small pieces.

4. Add a line of black stitching around the inside edge of the hoop (see Large Hoop step 8).

5. Finish the hoop neatly (see Large Hoop step 9).

> ✖ NOTE: *Hot-glue the ends of short, narrow ribbon in white or a coordinating color to the top of the hoops to make sweet hangers.*

NIGHT SKY MOBILE

DESIGNER ✖ LAURA HOWARD

MATERIALS & TOOLS

- ✖ Templates (page 112)

- ✖ Scissors

- ✖ 1 piece royal-blue felt, 9 x 12 inches (22.9 x 30.5 cm)

- ✖ 1 piece navy-blue felt, 9 x 12 inches (22.9 x 30.5 cm)

- ✖ 1 piece yellow felt, 8 x 8 inches (20.3 x 20.3 cm)

- ✖ 1 piece white felt, 8 x 8 inches (20.3 x 20.3 cm)

- ✖ Pins

- ✖ Sewing thread: 1 spool each in yellow and white

- ✖ Sewing needle

- ✖ Embroidery floss: 1 skein in white, separated into half-strands (i.e., for 6-stranded floss, split floss into two sections of 3 strands)

- ✖ 1 wooden embroidery hoop, 7 inches (18 cm) in diameter

- ✖ White acrylic craft paint

- ✖ Paintbrush and paint tray

- ✖ White yarn, 150 inches (381 cm)

- ✖ 1 sharp darning needle

- ✖ Ruler or measuring tape

Twinkly stars! A gleaming moon! Wisps of cloud drifting across the night sky as it darkens from dusk to midnight! This easy-to-sew mobile is inspired by the beautiful night sky. Want an even easier project? Skip the Blanket Stitch and instead sew the circles with Running Stitch and dark-blue sewing thread, then use "invisible" clear thread or fishing line to hang the circles.

Instructions

1. Use the templates provided (page 112) to cut out the following felt pieces: 10 yellow stars, 2 white moons, 6 white clouds, 9 royal-blue circles, and 9 navy-blue circles.

2. Each circle will be made up of two sides— 1 royal blue and 1 navy blue—and each side will be decorated with the same shaped cutout. Sew half the cutouts to royal-blue circles and half to navy-blue ones. To do so, position each cutout in the center of a circle and pin it in place. Sew the shapes to their backing felt with Running Stitch. Make sure to use threads that match in color (yellow or white). Remove the pins when finished.

3. Match the circles into pairs, and place each pair together, wrong sides facing. Make sure to line up the cutouts so they'll both be the right way up when the mobile is hanging. Using half strands of white embroidery floss, sew the edges of the circles together with Blanket Stitch. Start and finish at the top of each circle, and finish the stitching as neatly as possible.

4. Remove the inner ring from the wooden embroidery hoop. Paint the inner ring with two or three coats of white acrylic paint. Allow the paint to dry completely.

5. Cut a length of white yarn measuring approximately 50 inches (127 cm). Knot the yarn at one end and trim any excess yarn below the knot. Then use a sharp darning needle to thread upwards through three of the circles, making one strand of the mobile. Repeat this step to create the other two strands.

6. Now we'll attach the three strands to the painted hoop. One by one, loop the yarn strands around the hoop by bringing them through the hoop, then back around and through again. Adjust the yarn until the strands are equidistant from each other and hanging at your desired length. Knot the three strands at the top, trimming any excess. Use the yarn to hang the mobile.

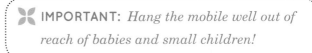
IMPORTANT: *Hang the mobile well out of reach of babies and small children!*

WHALE PILLOW & PHOTO PROP

DESIGNER ✳ LAURA HOWARD

Little ones grow so quickly! Record their progress with this project, which also doubles as a cute piece of nursery décor. Place the cushion on an armchair, attach the appropriate number and time (for example, 7 months), and sit your child beside the cushion for a mini photo shoot. With the detachable strips removed, the friendly whale can be a colorful feature of any nursery.

MATERIALS & TOOLS

✖ Templates (pages 113-116)

✖ Scissors

✖ 5 pieces white felt, each 9 x 12 inches (22.9 x 30.5 cm)

✖ 1 piece black felt, 7 x 8 inches (17.8 x 20.3 cm)

✖ 1 piece lilac-purple felt, 8 x 9 inches (20.3 x 22.9 cm)

✖ 1 piece orange felt, 2½ x 3 inches (6.4 x 7.6 cm)

✖ 1 piece blue felt, 15 x 15 inches (38 x 38 cm)

✖ 1 piece light-blue felt, 26 x 26 inches (66 x 66 cm)

✖ Ruler or flexible measuring tape

✖ Erasable fabric pen, pencil, or chalk

✖ Pins

✖ Sewing thread to match the felt colors, white, black, lilac, orange, blue, and light blue

✖ Sewing needle

✖ Embroidery floss: 1 skein in black

✖ White sew-on hook-and-loop tape, 38 inches (96.5 cm)

✖ Thimble (optional)

✖ Cushion insert/pad, 14 x 14 inches (35.6 x 35.6 cm)

✖ Thin tracing paper or tissue paper

✖ Fine pen

Instructions

1. Use the templates provided to cut out one water spurt and one eye from white felt, one eyeball from black felt, one whale and one whale tail from lilac felt, three large fish (Template A) and one small fish (Template B) from orange felt, and three waves from blue felt (one of each wave shape). Then turn over one of the large fish shapes so it's facing the opposite direction.

2. Measure and cut out three pieces of light-blue felt for the cushion: one measuring 14 x 14 inches (35.6 x 35.6 cm) and two measuring 9.5 x 14 inches (24.1 x 35.6 cm). Use a ruler and erasable fabric pen, pencil, or chalk to mark out the lines.

3. Arrange the waves, whale, and spurt on the square cushion piece (refer to the photos as a guide for positioning the pieces) and pin them in place. Sew the shapes to the backing felt with Whip Stitch and matching sewing threads while gradually removing the pins. Leave the outer edges of the square unstitched (figure A).

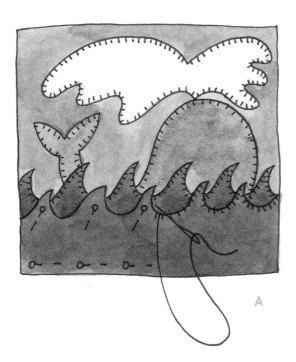

A

4. Add the whale's eye and eyeball, plus the four orange fish. Sew them in place one by one using Whip Stitch and matching threads. Start a new piece of thread for each fish; don't carry threads across the back of the work.

5. Cut a length of black embroidery floss and separate it into two pieces (for 6-stranded floss, split the floss into two sections of 3 strands each). Use this floss to stitch the whale's smile. Draw the smile on the felt with an erasable pen, pencil, or chalk, and then Backstitch along the line with small stitches. Also sew a few tiny overlapping stitches to create each of the fish's eyes.

6. Add two strips of hook-and-loop tape to the water spurt (refer to the photos as a guide). Cut one piece measuring 1½ inches (3.8 cm) and one measuring 4 inches (10.2 cm), and position them with a 1½ inch (3.8 cm) gap in between so they line up neatly, as pictured. Pin, then sew the tape in place using Whip Stitch and white sewing thread (figure B).

> ✿ NOTE: *It's important that you use the soft "loop" half of the hook-and-loop tape. Attaching the much softer "loop" strip to the cushion allows the cushion to be used comfortably without scratching.*

B

7. Arrange the three cushion pieces together to form an "envelope." Pin the layers together, then use light-blue sewing thread to Blanket Stitch around the edge, removing the pins gradually. When the cushion is completed, add the cushion insert/pad (figure C).

C

8. To make the number circles, use the templates provided to cut the number(s) from black felt and two circles from white felt. Position the numbers in the center of the backing circles, and sew them in place with black sewing thread and Whip Stitch.

9. To make each embroidered word (*month, months, year,* or *years*) trace the letters onto a piece of thin tracing paper or tissue paper with a fine pen. Allow the ink to dry completely, then pin the paper to a piece of white felt, making sure to leave room to cut out the full panel later. Use large Basting Stitches to hold the paper in place, then remove the pins. Embroider the letters with small Backstitches and half-strands of black embroidery floss (as in Step 5). When finished, remove the Basting Stitches and carefully tear away the paper from the stitching. Use pins to remove any remaining small pieces of paper (figure D).

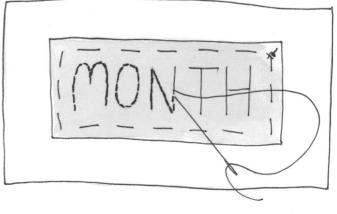

D

10. Trace the outline of the embroidered panel onto thin tracing paper or tissue paper, and cut it out. Arrange the panel over the stitched lettering so the word is in the center of the rectangle. Pin the template in place and cut out the panel, and then use the felt shape or the template to cut a matching backing piece from more white felt.

11. Add a strip of the hook side from the hook-and-loop tape to each numbered circle and embroidered panel. Cut a 1½ inch (3.8 cm) strip for each circle, a 4-inch (10.2 cm) strip for the times, and a 7-inch (17.8 cm) strip for the name. One by one, hold each strip in place in the center of the backing circle/panel and sew it in position with Whip Stitch and white sewing thread.

12. Sew the two circles and the two embroidered panels together, right sides facing out, using Blanket Stitch and more white sewing thread. When sewing the circles, make sure the number and the hook strip are properly aligned so that when you attach the circle to the cushion, the number will be straight.

IMPORTANT: *This is not a toy! Supervise babies and very young children around the detachable pieces, and remove them when the cushion is not in use as a photo prop (or display it well out of their reach).*

TIP: *It's important that you use the "hook" half of the tape for all these pieces so they will attach to the "loop" strips added to the cushion.*

SCALLOPED FELT STORAGE BOXES

DESIGNER ✖ VALERIE LLOYD

These small square boxes are perfect for storage and organization in the nursery. They are made from soft felt with Blanket-Stitched corners and are reinforced with cardboard to hold up to daily use. The boxes can be arranged on shelves, used for changing table organization, or even placed inside dresser drawers to separate clothing items.

MATERIALS & TOOLS

- ✖ Solid-colored felt, ½ yard (.46 m)
- ✖ Scissors
- ✖ Ruler or flexible measuring tape
- ✖ Erasable fabric pen, pencil, or chalk
- ✖ Sewing pins
- ✖ Heavy-duty thread
- ✖ Large sewing needle
- ✖ Felt in contrasting color, ¼ yard (.23 m)
- ✖ Pinking shears
- ✖ Glue gun and glue cartridges
- ✖ 4 squares scrap cardboard, 4¼ inches (10.8 cm)

Instructions

1. Cut out two 15-inch (38.1-cm) squares of felt, and stack them one on top of the other.

2. Use a ruler and chalk (or another erasable method) to mark 5-inch (12.7-cm) squares in all four corners. Cut along the chalk lines through both layers of felt, and remove the four corners. The resulting pieces of felt will be shaped like a plus sign.

3. With the layers of felt still stacked together, bring the adjacent sides up and pin them together to create the corners of the box (figure A).

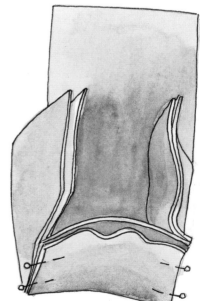

A

4. Thread a large needle with doubled heavy-duty thread. Knot the end. Begin a Blanket Stitch at the bottom of a corner, working up to the top of the box. Work to keep the stitches evenly spaced all the way up the corner of the box. At the top of the box, knot the thread, and cut the tails short. Sew all four corners of the box, securing all layers of felt with a Blanket Stitch (figure B).

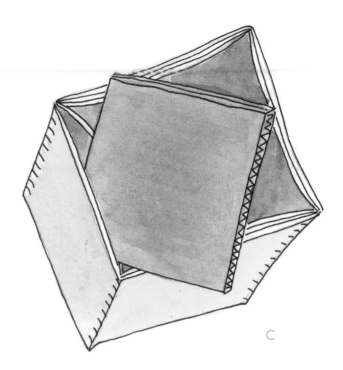

C

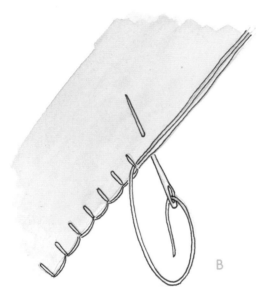

B

5. Slide a square of cardboard into the pocket between the layers of felt on each side of the box (figure C).

6. Cut out a long strip of felt in a contrasting color measuring 2⅝ x 22 inches (6.7 x 55.9 cm). Use the template (page 111) to trace the scallop pattern with chalk on one edge of the strip. Cut along the chalk lines using pinking shears to give it a decorative edge. Then cut along the straight edge of the strip with pinking shears.

7. Use a ruler to make a chalk line along the length of the scalloped strip 1 inch (2.5 cm) from the straight edge. Starting at one end of the scalloped strip, use a glue gun to run a bead of glue roughly the length of one side of the box along the chalk line. Lay the top edge of the box on the line of glue and press to secure. Add another bead of glue, turn the box, and apply the strip to the next side of the box. Continue until all sides of the box have the scalloped trim attached. Cut off the excess trim, and glue at the corner where the ends of the trim meet.

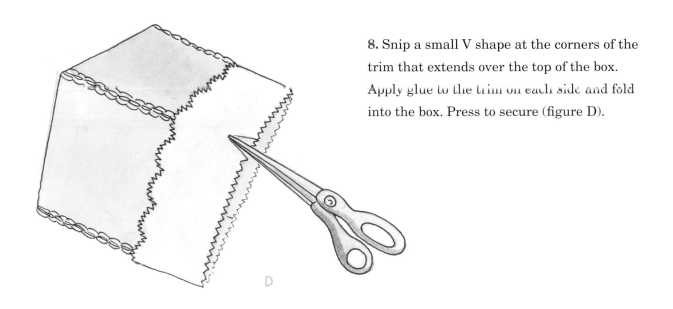

8. Snip a small V shape at the corners of the trim that extends over the top of the box. Apply glue to the trim on each side and fold into the box. Press to secure (figure D).

ELEGANT FOOTPRINT PLAQUE

DESIGNER ✖ VALERIE LLOYD

For this charming keepsake, an ink print is taken from baby's foot and af-
fixed to a wooden plaque with upholstery tacks. Metallic gold accents and
a ribbon hanger turn this simple decoration into a cherished heirloom.

MATERIALS & TOOLS

✖ Water-soluble ink pad in the color
of your choice

✖ Light-colored, heavy-weight paper

✖ Scissors

✖ Glue stick

✖ Oval wooden plaque, 5 x 7 inches
(12.7 x 17.8 cm)

✖ Upholstery tacks

✖ Hammer

✖ Metallic gold paint

✖ Paintbrush

✖ Picture-hanging D-Rings with
hardware

✖ Ribbon in the color of your choice,
2 yards (1.8 m)

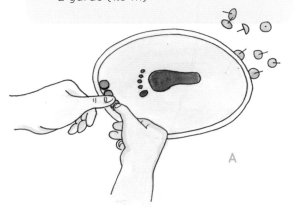

A

Instructions

1. With the baby lying on its back on the floor, press
an ink pad against his or her foot, and then apply a
sheet of paper to capture the footprint. Press each
toe against the paper to get a clean print. Make
several prints, and then choose the best one to make
into the plaque.

2. Cut the print to fit inside the oval shape of the
plaque with the footprint at the center. Use a glue
stick to apply the print to the plaque, and set a
weight or stack of books on top of the print until the
glue has dried.

3. Use decorative upholstery tacks to create a border
around the outside of the print. Begin applying each
tack by pressing it into the wood with your thumb to
get the positioning right, and then tap it all the way
in with a hammer (figure A).

4. Paint the edges of the plaque with metallic gold
paint. Let dry.

5. Attach two picture frame D-rings on the back of
the plaque, near the sides. Run a length of ribbon
through the rings and tie into a bow a few inches
above the top of the plaque. Hang the plaque on the
wall from a nail.

YARN-WRAPPED NAME SIGN

DESIGNER ✕ VALERIE LLOYD

This modern decoration is made using yarn-wrapped wire, which is bent to form baby's name in cursive script. It's framed using an embroidery hoop wrapped with yarn in a coordinating color.

MATERIALS & TOOLS

✕ Embroidery hoop, 12 inches (30.5 cm) in diameter

✕ Large sheet of paper

✕ Pencil

✕ Two colors of yarn

✕ Scissors

✕ Scrap cardboard

✕ 16-gauge vine-coated floral wire

✕ Wire cutters

✕ Pliers

✕ Clothespins or binder clips

✕ Masking tape

> ✕ **TIP:** *For letters with dots, like lowercase i or j, draw an outline of the dot and connect it to the lower part of the letter.*

Instructions

1. Remove the outer ring of the embroidery hoop. Only the inner ring will be used to make the sign. Lay the hoop on a large sheet of paper and trace around the inside with a pencil to make a guide for the name sign. Inside the drawn ring, write baby's name in cursive script. Write it using one line, without starts or stops. The name needs to connect to both sides of the circle, so add tails to the first and last letters so that they touch the circle.

2. Cut a long piece of yarn and loosely lay it over the name, including areas where the line of the letters doubles back on itself. Measure the length of that piece of yarn, and add 8 inches (20.3 cm). This is the amount of wire needed to complete the name (figure A).

A

3. Wrap yarn around a roughly 2 x 4 inch (5.1 x 10.2 cm) piece of cardboard to make a handheld paddle. Begin wrapping the wire at one end. Lay the tail of the yarn along the length of the wire a few inches and then wrap the wire and the yarn tail together, trapping it securely. Tightly wind the yarn around the wire, completely covering it (figure B). Continue until the entire wire is covered in yarn. To tie off the end, make a loop of yarn, slip the end of the wire through, and pull tight.

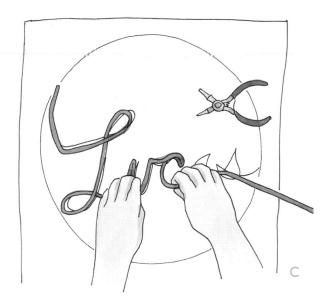

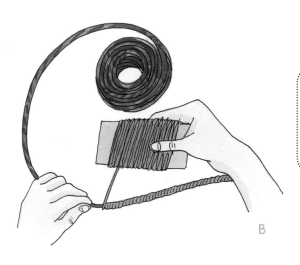

4. Begin forming the wire into the first letter of the name. Leave 4 inches (10.2 cm) at the beginning—this will connect to the hoop later. Bend the wire one small section at a time and use pliers to make corners sharp. Check the letters against the written template frequently to match it up as closely as possible. At the end of the name, leave another 4-inch (10.2-cm) length of wire for attaching to the hoop (figure C).

TIP: *For letters where the line crosses itself or meets, a clothespin or binder clip can be helpful; this will hold completed letters in place while the rest are formed.*

5. Turn the name over. Use short bits of yarn to tie loose areas together, like where the line of a letter doubles back or crosses another section. Tie a tight knot and trim the ends so that the knot isn't visible from the front. Use these little ties to strengthen and secure any areas that may lose shape once the sign is hung on the wall (figure D).

6. Set the name into the embroidery hoop and connect the 4-inch ends to the hoop with wrappings of masking tape.

7. Load the cardboard paddle with the other color of yarn and use it to wrap the entire hoop. Hang the name sign on the wall with a small finishing nail.

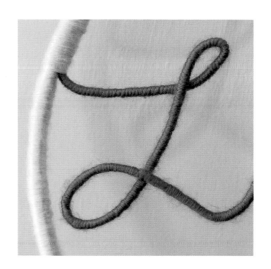

D

PROJECT TEMPLATES

EMBROIDERED LINEN BIB
Page 75 — Enlarge by 160%

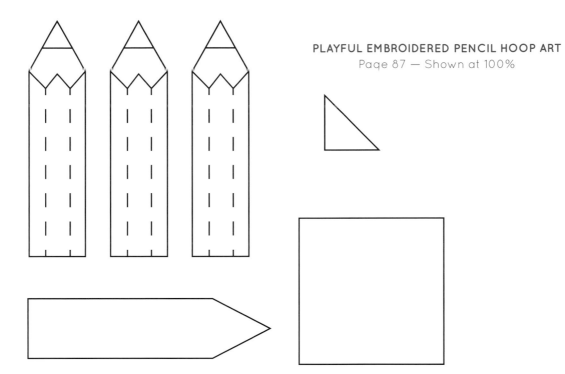

PLAYFUL EMBROIDERED PENCIL HOOP ART
Page 87 — Shown at 100%

SCALLOPED FELT STORAGE BOXES
Page 101 — Shown at 100%

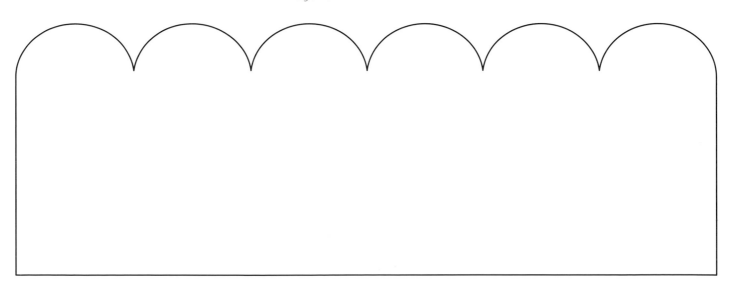

WHALE PILLOW & PHOTO PROP
Page 95— Enlarge by 200%

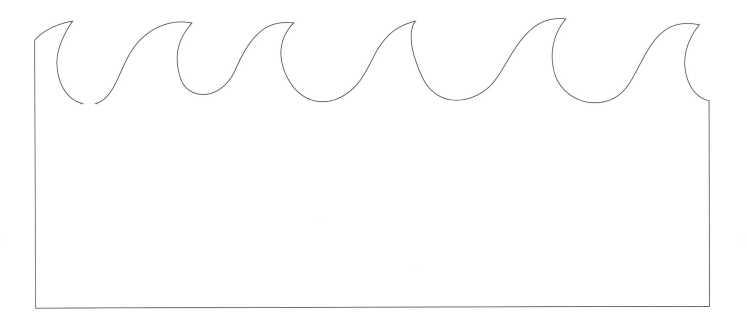

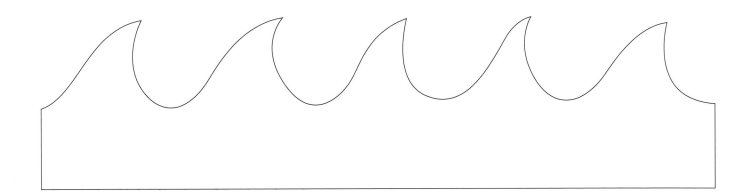

A

B

WHALE PILLOW & PHOTO PROP
Page 95 — Enlarge by 160%

Enlarge by 200%

MONTHS

YEARS

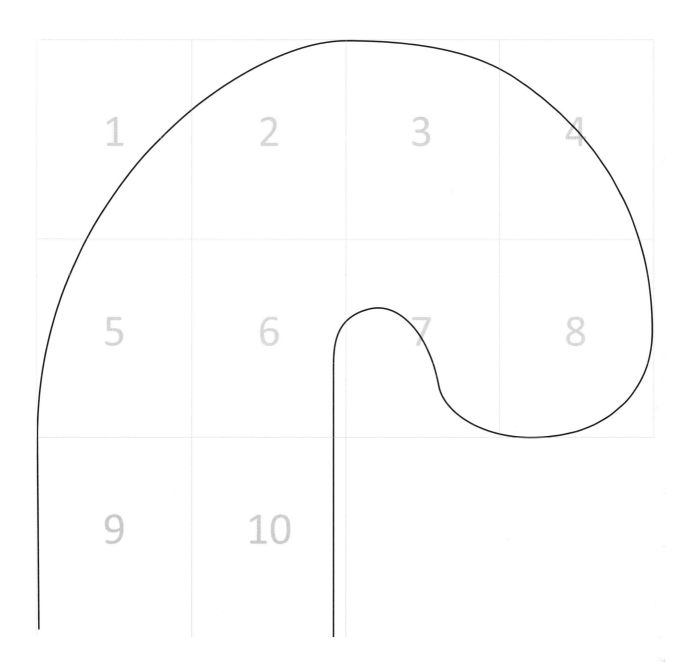

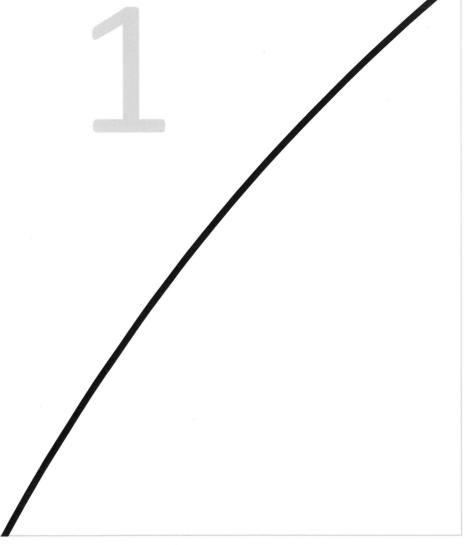

MATERNITY PILLOW
Page 51 — Shown at 100%

2

3

MATERNITY PILLOW
Page 51 — Shown at 100%

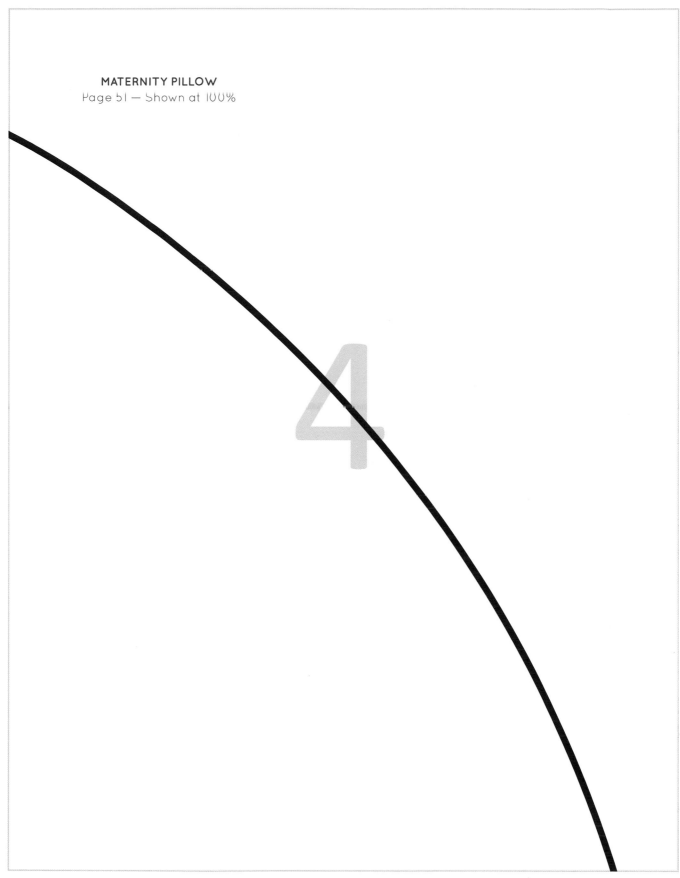

5

MATERNITY PILLOW
Page 51 — Shown at 100%

6

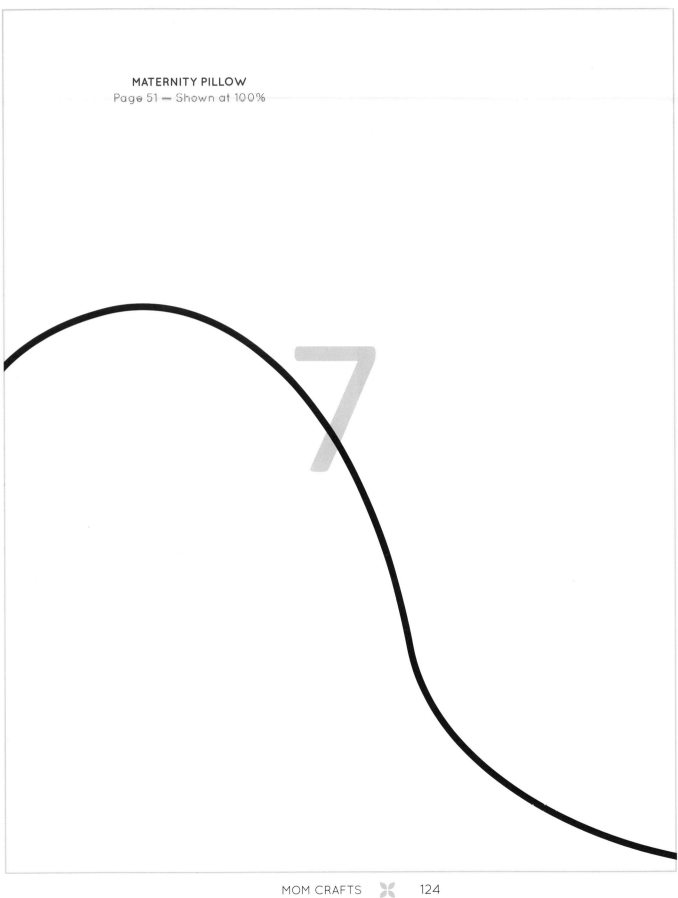

MATERNITY PILLOW
Page 51 — Shown at 100%

8

9

MATERNITY PILLOW
Page 51 — Shown at 100%

10

BITTY BEAR DIAPER BAG TAG
Page 73 — Shown at 100%

BABY ANIMAL BURP CLOTHS
Page 69 — Enlarge by 160%

RAINBOW BABY SLING
Page 59 — Enlarge by 160%

TUMMY TIME FLOOR QUILT
Page 65 — Shown at 100%

ABOUT THE DESIGNERS

EMILIE AKKERMANS

Emilie Akkermans was born and raised in Canada. She was inspired to launch her own start-up crafting business, Emilie Creations, after living in many countries and traveling extensively. She finds inspiration for her creations in the cultures, languages, and trends she observes during her travels and uses these influences in her current pursuits of clothing, furniture, surface, and bag design. Emilie currently lives in Uruguay with her husband and their two dogs. To learn more about Emilie and view her latest creations, visit her Emilie Creations Etsy and Facebook pages.

JESSICA FEDIW

As a wife and devoted mother of two, Jessica has traveled throughout the East Coast and Gulf states, splitting her time and energy between raising a young family and channeling her creative passions. Early on, Jessica began sewing as a way to make one-of-a-kind outfits for her daughter. She took to blogging online and founded *Happy Together* (www.happytogetherbyjess.com) to capture her journey and share her experiences with others. Eventually, she expanded her creative interests to much more than just sewing. Jessica is influencing others around the world with the message that love, family, and happiness is found when we share life together.

THERESA GROSH

Inspired by her thrifty, seamstress, Mennonite ancestors, Theresa Grosh finds great joy in turning vintage, handmade linens from yesteryear into new products that can be enjoyed by modern folks. Theresa's crafting business, Naptime Inspirations, can be found at www.naptimeinspirations.etsy.com and on Facebook. When not sewing and singing show tunes in her studio, Theresa can be found gardening, reading, or enjoying time with her husband and four talented daughters in rural Lancaster County, Pennsylvania.

LAURA HOWARD

Laura is a designer/maker and crafts writer living near London, England. She loves to make stuff, especially if it involves her favorite material: felt! She regularly contributes projects to craft books and magazines, and she's the author of two books about felt crafting: *Super-Cute Felt* (and *Super-Cute Felt Animals*. Laura shares free tutorials and writes about her crafty adventures on her blog, bugsandfishes.blogspot.com, and sells her work at lupin.etsy.com.

MOLLIE JOHANSON

Mollie Johanson has loved cute things, creative messes, and cuddly critters for as long as she can remember. Her blog, *Wild Olive,* is known for embroidery patterns, simply stitched projects, and playful printables, most often featuring charming creations with smiling faces. She is the author of *Stitch Love: Sweet Creatures Big & Small,* and she regularly contributes to a variety of magazines and books, including several Lark Crafts titles. Mollie lives near Chicago and is happiest with a cup of coffee, some stitching, and her family close at hand.

VALERIE LLOYD

Valerie Lloyd is no stranger to glittery messes and hot glue "situations." After achieving success with her Etsy shop, Smile Mercantile, Valerie launched smilemercantile.com, where she sells specialty craft supplies and seasonal decorations. When not crafting up a storm, she enjoys photography, tending her garden, or hunting for vintage treasures at thrift stores and estate sales. Valerie lives in Seattle with her husband, Khris, and their cat, Bentley.

CAROL J. SULCOSKI

Carol J. Sulcoski is an attorney turned knitting designer, author, hand dyer, and teacher. She is author of *Lace Yarn Studio*; *Sock Yarn Studio*; *Knitting Socks With Handpainted Yarns* and co-author of *Knit So Fine: Knitting With Skinny Yarns*. Her designs have been published in *Vogue Knitting, Interweave Knits, Creative Knitting Magazine, Noro Magazine*, and other books and magazines. Her technical articles also frequently appear in premier knitting magazines like *Vogue Knitting*. She is the founder of Black Bunny Fibers (www.blackbunnyfibers.com), a boutique hand-dyeing business selling unique yarns, fibers, and patterns. She lives outside Philadelphia with her family.

TESS & RAE

Tess & Rae is a Melbourne, Australia-based business set up by two mums who share a passion for fabric, sewing, bags, and accessories. Tess and Rae are two friends with like minds and two kids each. They established in 2013 after being inspired to create fun, vibrant, and functional accessories for women and children. They know the importance of functionality in an item from experience—especially when one has kids, but they also wanted to incorporate some fresh and vibrant patterns into designs. They can be found online at tessandrae.com.au, Etsy, Facebook, and Instagram.

INDEX

Note: Page numbers in *italics* indicate projects and (templates). Page numbers in **bold** indicate designer bios.

R

Rainbow Baby Sling, *59–61* (*129*)

Room decor. *See* Nursery projects

Rotary cutter and mat, 4

Running stitch, 25

S

Satin stitch, 26

Scalloped Felt Storage Boxes, *101–103* (*111*)

Scallop stitch, 26

Scarf, lightweight nursing infinity, *39*

Scissors, 5

Seam allowances, 15

Seam ripper, 4

Seams, pressing, 15

Sewing

    needles, 4

    scissors, 5

    threads, 9

Sewing machine, 4–5

    needles, 4

    stitches, 25

    stitching with, 13

    threads, 9

    vinyl sewing tip, 11

Skirt, maternity, *55–57*

Sling, baby, *59–61* (*129*)

Slip, slip, knit (SSK), 21

Snaps, 7

SSK (slip, slip, knit), 21

Stitches, embroidery

    French knot, 25–26

    satin stitch, 26

    scallop stitch, 26

Stitches, hand-sewing

    backstitch, 23

    basting stitch, 23

    blanket stitch, 24

    ladder stitch, 24

    running stitch, 25

    whip stitch, 25

Stitches, machine

    about: using machine for, 13

    edgestitch, 25

    topstitch, 25

    zigzag stitch, 25

Stockinette stitch (St st), 22

Storage boxes, scalloped felt, *101–103* (*111*)

Straps, making and attaching, 13

Strawberry Hat & Booties, *79–83*

Stretch knit, 10

Stretch markings, 15

St st (stockinette stitch), 22

Stuffing/layering materials, 8–9

Sulcoski, Carol J., *79–83*, **131**

T

Tacks, upholstery, 7

Tag, diaper bag, *73–74* (*128*)

Tape, masking, 9

Techniques

    binding with bias tape, 11–12

    clipping corners, 12

    clipping/notching curves, 12

    corners, 5

    embroidery transfers, 12–13

    knitting, 17–22

    machine stitching, 13

    making bias tape, 14

    piecing/patchwork, 14

    pressing seams, 15

    quilting guidelines, 15

    seam allowances, 15

    strap construction and attachment, 13

    stretch markings, 15

    using templates, 15

Templates. *See also specific projects*

    for projects, 108–129

    using, 15

Tess & Rae, *45–49*, **132**

Threader, 4

Threads, 9

Tissue paper, 9

Tools and materials, 3–10

    fabric, 9–10

    materials, 5–9

    tools, 3–5, 6

Topstitch, 25

Tracing paper, 9

Transferring patterns, 12–13

Tummy Time Floor Quilt, *65–68 (129)*

U

Upholstery fabric, 10

Upholstery tacks, 7

V

Velcro (hook-and-loop closure), 8

Vinyl, 10–11

W

Whale Pillow & Photo Prop, *95–99 (113–116)*

Whip stitch, 25

Wire cutters, 6

Wire, floral, 6

Wooden plaques, 7

Wool, 10

Y

Yarn-Wrapped Name Sign, *107–109*

Z

Zigzag stitch, 25

Zippers, 9